POEMS

ON LIFE AND LOVE IN

ANCIENT INDIA

SUNY SERIES IN HINDU STUDIES

Wendy Doniger, editor

Poems on Life and Love in
Ancient India

Hāla's *Sattasaī*

Translated from the Prakrit and Introduced by

PETER KHOROCHE

and

HERMAN TIEKEN

excelsior editions
AN IMPRINT OF STATE UNIVERSITY OF NEW YORK PRESS

Published by
STATE UNIVERSITY OF NEW YORK PRESS
ALBANY

© 2009 State University of New York
All rights reserved
Printed in the United States of America

No part of this book may be used or reproduced in any manner whatsoever without written permission. No part of this book may be stored in a retrieval system or transmitted in any form or by any means including electronic, electrostatic, magnetic tape, mechanical, photocopying, recording, or otherwise without the prior permission in writing of the publisher.

For information, contact
State University of New York Press, Albany, NY
www.sunypress.edu

Production and book design, Laurie Searl
Marketing, Michael Campochiaro

Library of Congress Cataloging-in-Publication Data

Hāla.
 [Gathasaptasati. English]
 Poems on life and love in ancient India : Hāla's Sattasaī / translated from the Prakrit and introduced by Peter Khoroche and Herman Tieken.
   p. cm. — (SUNY series in Hindu studies)
 Includes bibliographical references and index.
 ISBN 978-0-7914-9391-5 (hardcover : alk. paper)
 ISBN 978-0-7914-9392-2 (pbk. : alk. paper)
 1. Love poetry, Prakrit—Translations into English. 2. Prakrit poetry—Translations into English. 3. Hāla—Translations into English. I. Khoroche, Peter. II. Tieken, Herman Joseph Hugo, 1952– III. Title. IV. Title: Hāla's Sattasaī.
 PK5013.H3G313 2009
 891'.3—dc22

2009005435

10 9 8 7 6 5 4 3 2 1

CONTENTS

VII   ACKNOWLEDGMENT
I   INTRODUCTION

The Poems

15   INVITATION
17   EXCHANGING GLANCES
29   LOVERS' MEETINGS
39   WRONG CHOICES AND DISAPPOINTMENTS
51   THE GO-BETWEEN
55   THE YOUNG COUPLE
65   MAKING LOVE
83   THE PERFECT WIFE
87   THE BROTHER-IN-LAW
91   RIVAL WIVES
95   THE ERRANT HUSBAND
103   GETTING HER NAME WRONG
105   LOVERS' QUARRELS
125   THE FAITHLESS WIFE
131   THE ABDUCTED WIFE
133   DEPARTURE
137   THE TRAVELER'S WIFE
153   THE TRAVELER
161   COUNTRY CHARACTERS
175   GODS AND SAINTS
179   THE GOD OF LOVE

183	ALLEGORICAL VERSES
189	POETIC FANCY
197	GOOD MEN AND BAD
201	EPILOGUE
205	VARIANT READINGS
207	CONCORDANCE
211	BIBLIOGRAPHY

ACKNOWLEDGMENT

We would like to thank the Gonda Foundation which generously made it possible for us to complete our translation in the summer of 2006 under the auspices of the International Institute for Asian Studies in Leiden.

INTRODUCTION

I

The *Sattasaī*, or The Seven Hundred, is an anthology of short poems about love and marriage in the villages of the Indian countryside. The selection is attributed to the Sātavāhana king Hāla, who reigned briefly in the first century AD in what is now the state of Maharashtra. The poems are indeed set in this part of peninsular India, whose northern boundary, the Vindhya Hills, and whose rivers, the Godāvarī and Narmadā, they frequently mention. But the first-century dating is probably much too early and the connection with Hāla most likely a literary fiction. These are points to which we will return.

All the poems are couplets and nearly all are in the musical *āryā* meter, which allows a variety of rhythm within its eight "bars." Though their form is ultimately derived from song, they were not necessarily intended to be sung. The language of the poems is Prakrit. This is a general term for any dialect of Sanskrit, itself the language par excellence of sacred texts and official documents in ancient India. The Prakrit in question is a stylized imitation of the language spoken by country people living south of the Vindhyas, an area that for long remained beyond the pale of North Indian Sanskrit culture. Compared with Sanskrit, which is free of recognizably local elements, the language of the *Sattasaī* is intended to convey a rustic, Maharashtrian flavor. Even so, it remains no less a literary language than Sanskrit.

Within its brief compass each separate, self-contained poem describes an emotion or presents a situation, often obliquely. Frequently it takes the form of a monologue: we hear someone, usually a woman, addressing her friend, her mother or some older female relative, her lover, her husband or simply herself. Occasionally there is dialogue, or else the speaker gives advice or warning to a young girl or boy inexperienced in the ways of the world. Practically all the poems are in one way or another about love, though the application may not always be obvious in what appear to be general maxims or straightforward descriptions of nature or the seasons.

The poems about love's joys and love's excesses are notable for their frankness but, as with all love poetry, the greater part of the *Sattasaī* is about unhappy love: love thwarted, unrequited, dissembled or betrayed, as well as love in separation. While still unmarried, a young girl is kept under close watch by her parents to guard her reputation. She needs considerable daring and ingenuity to make secret assignations with her lover in the fields and forests surrounding the village, and such meetings are always at the mercy of the changing seasons: the harvest robs the fields of cover, sheltering trees lose their leaves. Married life brings a new set of problems, beginning with the many misunderstandings between the husband and his new bride, who are usually complete strangers to one another. After the wedding the young wife becomes part of the large household of her husband's family. Her mother-in-law bosses her about, her husband's younger brothers pester her, and she is in fierce competition with her husband's other wives for his favor. All too soon her husband loses interest in her and turns to other women. She can only retaliate by sulking. Even when the marriage is a happy one, the husband is often away from home on long business trips. Though he may suffer hardships, the fate of the lonely wife left behind is harsher still. She is pictured as inconsolable in her misery.

2

To appreciate the poems fully it is essential to understand their tone and intention. The scenes and the characters may be rustic but the verses are anything but homespun. In the second poem of the collection the *Sattasaī* is explicitly contrasted with a wholly different literature about love:

> Shame on those who cannot appreciate
> This ambrosial Prakrit poetry
> But pore instead
> Over treatises on love.

The earliest known treatise on love is the *Kāmasūtra,* which probably dates from the third century AD. It is in Sanskrit and in prose, and its highly theoretical approach to love and sex is at the opposite extreme from that of the *Sattasaī.* Here everything is docketed and programed. For example, in a chapter dealing with nail scratching as part of love play, eight different-shaped nail marks are listed (each with its suggestive name: the Gooseflesh, the Half-Moon, the Circle, the Line, the Tiger's Claw, the Peacock's Foot, the Hare's Leap and the Lotus Leaf) as well as six places on the body where they are to be applied. This is followed by a categorization of nails into long, short and medium (medium being best as combining the qualities of both long and short). Then come detailed directions: the Gooseflesh is made by moving nails of medium length lightly over the woman's chin, breasts and lower lip without leaving any trace. The Half-Moon is a curved mark left by the nails on the neck or the upper part of the breasts. And so on. In the end, though, as if acknowledging the futility of such prescriptions, the treatise allows that the lover may also make other scratches of whatever shape he likes. Compare, on the subject of half-moons, poem 261 with its allusion to the amorous propensities of brothers-in-law:

> My dear man,
> Why scan the sky
> If it's crescent moons you're after?
> Try looking at your sister-in-law's shoulder:
> You'll find a whole row of them there.

The *Kāmasūtra* is concerned essentially with classification: it gives names to things and enumerates them, claiming that to know these enables one to act in a way that will ensure the highest possible gratification. It is not a handbook on sex but a compendium of the endless variety of situations one may encounter in one's sexual life. Success is then merely a matter of avoiding the ones which are least likely to lead to gratification. But this process requires a just assessment of one's own experience and desire as well as those of one's partner. And, as shown in the *Sattasaī* time and again, this is precisely where things tend to go wrong. Take poem 158 about a newly wed couple:

> He was embarrassed
> But I laughed and gave him a hug
> When he groped for the knot
> Of my skirt and found it
> Already undone.

This scene may be compared with the chapter in the *Kāmasūtra* entitled "Winning a Virgin's Trust," which explains how the husband should win over his inexperienced wife in a series of simple steps, beginning by gently taking her on his lap and ending by loosening the knot of her skirt. The objections the wife might make at each step are adduced together with the ways the husband is to counter them. It is much the same as practicing swimming on dry land. The realities of life are quite different, as in the above poem, where the husband miscalculates his partner's bashfulness.

The *Kāmasūtra* and the *Sattasaī* represent two totally different views of love and sex. In the *Kāmasūtra* everything imaginable is considered and treated as equally relevant: it is the product of an ingenious but academic mind. The *Sattasaī*, by contrast, provides an endless number of examples showing the futility of the *Kāmasūtra*'s lists and enumerations. Where the *Kāmasūtra* is concerned with theory, the *Sattasaī* confronts this theory with the untidy reality of life. The opposition between the two works is so striking as to seem intentional, especially in view of the explicit contrast made in poem 2. That contrast can be further highlighted if we compare the typically thwarted lover of the *Sattasaī* with the *beau ideal* of the *Kāmasūtra*, who can perform all the tricks in the book and is no village yokel. We are given a full description of this townsman's sumptuous mansion and of his daily round of pleasures: picnics, parties, poetry readings and prostitutes. Conspicuously absent from his timetable is work: clearly he is a man of means and belongs to the leisured class. But he is also well-educated—after years of study he has mastered the complicated grammar and large vocabulary of Sanskrit—and he is a man of parts: he can sing, make music on the rims of glasses, play the lute, arrange flowers, tell jokes and riddles, discuss architecture and improvise poems, besides being something of an athlete. In short, he is the perfectly accomplished man, at home in a salon or any social gathering. He lives, if not in the capital, at least in a city or market town. The description of this *nāgaraka*, or "townsman," ends by recounting what happens when he attempts to live the life of a townsman in a village. Predictably he runs into difficulties when he tries to organize a reading group. He is then advised to entice the curious to his salon by describing to them the sort of extravagant party a *nāgaraka* like himself lays on. Another suggestion is that he should bribe the villagers to attend his gatherings.

Each figure, the unhappy lover from the village and the successful lover from the town, is to some extent a caricature: the idealized *nāgaraka* is even more unreal than the villager. But the image of the one seems to have been shaped by that of the other, in that the contrast between them was deliberately exaggerated. It seems very likely that the *Sattasaī* and the *Kāmasūtra* originated in the same milieu and at about the same period. The poems should therefore be read with the townsman, his lifestyle and his accomplishments in mind. It is then a question of how far one should push this contrast. In such obviously amusing scenes as the one in which the husband fails to recognize an experienced woman in his young bride it works and the resultant humor is gentle. But in a poem such as the following there is a problem of interpretation:

> Though he had no more work in the fields,
> The farmer would not go home,
> To spare himself the pain
> Of finding it empty
> Now that his wife was dead   [556]

At first sight this is a touching description of bereavement (and there are other poems in the anthology which treat this theme unambiguously, e.g., 557). But if we read it from the *nāgaraka*'s viewpoint it is possible to detect a cruel twist. The townsman depicted in the *Kāmasūtra,* unlike the farmer in the poem, is not dependent only on his wife for female company, as he is constantly surrounded by sophisticated courtesans. He can also afford to support more than one wife. Though such a *sous entendre* may go against our own romantic or sentimental notions, the possibility of its presence should at least be borne in mind.

3

Another problem of interpretation is posed by those poems which appear to be purely descriptive or else are in the form of general maxims. Since the *Sattasaī* is essentially an anthology of love poems, should erotic connotations, however remote, be sought in these too? Take the following:

> Lotuses know that winter is hot
> Because it makes them wilt.
> However much they try to hide their true nature
> People are betrayed by their acts.   [686]

Ostensibly this is a maxim, expressed in typically paradoxical fashion. But, in view of the last line, it may be possible to see in it a comment on an unfaithful lover or husband. The erotic connection is even harder to detect in this poetic fancy:

> With cooing doves hidden high up in the rafters
> The temple groans like a man suffering from cramp.   [652]

The commentaries on the *Sattasaī*, which date from approximately the thirteenth to the sixteenth centuries, take such poems as coded messages between lovers. Here, according to one of them, a woman is telling her lover that the temple is empty and is an ideal rendezvous. They need not be anxious about being noisy while making love. People will just think it is the doves. A similarly far-fetched interpretation is offered for the following conceit:

> Hear how that cloud groans with the effort,
> Yet is unable to lift the earth
> With ropes of raindrops
> That fall in unbroken streams. [665]

Here too a commentator falls back on the stock explanation that a woman is reassuring her lover that, as it is pelting with rain, no one is going to disturb the rendezvous they have planned. Not much is gained by such strained "explanations," and it would seem best to accept this poem as a highly fanciful description of rain. Its connection with the main topic of the anthology seems to lie in the very important role played by the rainy season in people's love lives (see poems 486 ff.). In some cases, though, the interpretation offered by the commentators is apt. It makes sense to assume, as they do, that the following words, addressed to an "ungrateful" honey bee, were spoken by a pregnant wife within earshot of her absconding husband:

> Ungrateful bee,
> Once you would not think
> Of enjoying yourself with other flowers
> But now that the jasmine is heavy with fruit
> You forsake her. [615]

In many cases a poem stands in no need of any explanation. The following, with its highly erotic image, is best left to speak for itself:

> Look!
> A tender shoot has sprouted from the stone of a ripe mango.
> It looks like an eel hiding in a half-opened oyster shell. [658]

The commentators are not necessarily unanimous in their solutions to what they regard as the riddles posed by the poems. Poem 228 may serve as an example:

> "Take it and have a look!"
> With a broad smile on her face
> She hands her husband the jujube fruit
> With the marks on it
> Of their son's first pair of teeth.

At one level it may be read as a charming scene in the life of a young family. But in the predominantly erotic context of the *Sattasaī* one would be right to look for a subtext. One commentator explains the mother's joy by the fact that the baby can now be weaned and she and her husband need no longer abstain from sex. The tooth marks on the fruit may be seen as an invitation—"Come, bite me!"—to her husband. Another commentator goes a step further by suggesting that it is not the infant who has implanted the tooth marks but the wife in her impatience to have sex.

4

In the third poem the compilation of the *Sattasaī* is attributed to Hāla:

> Among countless elegant poems,
> King Hāla, patron of poets,
> Has selected seven hundred.

Hāla was a king of the South Indian Sātavāhana dynasty, whose brief reign is placed somewhere in the first century AD. This date now seems too early for the *Sattasaī*, if we link it with its complementary antitype, the *Kāmasūtra*, which dates from the second half of the third century at the earliest. It is significant that the literary tradition itself seems to contradict Hāla's role as compiler of the anthology. In some manuscripts of the text each poem has the name of its supposed author appended to it. Most of the poets are otherwise unknown, but among the few names that can be identified we find, beside Hāla himself, a number of kings belonging to dynasties later than the Sātavāhanas. All these names were most probably added at a relatively advanced stage of the transmission of the text, on the model of much later Sanskrit anthologies, so as to give the collection greater credence. What is striking is that all these later kings belong to dynasties, such as the Vākāṭakas and Rāṣṭrakūṭas, which succeeded the Sātavāhanas in South India between the second and the fifth centuries. These attributions, however fictitious, reinforce the idea of the *Sattasaī*'s origin in South India, and this same idea seems to lie behind the attribution of the work to a Sātavāhana king of the first century. This also fits perfectly the fictional setting of the poems south of the Vindhyas, in peninsular India. The Vindhya Hills formed a boundary between the traditional heartland of Sanskrit culture in the north of India and the south, which was colonized only gradually. Although it was under the Sātavāhanas that North Indian culture was first introduced into South India on anything like a large scale, in their inscriptions the Sātavāhanas used Prakrit not Sanskrit. The situation is mirrored in a literary legend according to which the first Sātavāhana kings were ignoramuses, who could not speak Sanskrit. This appears to have led to misunderstandings with their wives, who were imported from the north. To northerners the people of the south, including their kings, seemed like hillbillies.

As regards the attribution of the *Sattasaī* to Hāla in particular among the thirty or so known kings of the Sātavāhana dynasty, one should note that his name evokes the word for plow, *hala*, a derivation of which, *halia* "plowman," is frequently used in the *Sattasaī* to refer to the farmer. It may have been felt appropriate that a collection of poems about village life should be attributed to a king whose name could be interpreted as meaning "Superplowman."

It nevertheless remains difficult to assign an exact date to the *Sattasaī*. All one can say is that the anthology clearly originated in a sophisticated literary milieu which also, and possibly simultaneously, produced the *Kāmasūtra*, and that it was most probably compiled sometime between the third century and the seventh, when we find the first reference to it in Bāṇa's preface to his *Harṣacarita* (c. 640).

5

The *Sattasaī* was always very popular in literary circles. Manuscripts of it are to be found all over India. There are also numerous commentaries dating from the thirteenth century onwards, that is, several centuries after the presumed date of its composition. In a way the work has suffered from its popularity. For one thing, with each handwritten copy new scribal errors crept into the text. This was aggravated by its being in Prakrit, a language not fixed and codified in the way Sanskrit was. In addition, the situations described, or alluded to, in the poems were not always properly understood, and as a result the text was altered or whole poems simply scrapped. But every poem that was deleted had to be replaced by a new one to make up the full number of seven hundred, which had at some point become the canonical number. As a result the first critical edition of the *Sattasaī*, produced in 1881 by Albrecht Weber and based on seventeen manuscripts, contains no fewer than 964 poems, of which only 430 are common to all versions.

The order of the verses varies in the different recensions. Originally there may have been no systematic ordering by content, but some later recensions group the verses in sections according to topic, situation or poetic figure, following the practice of contemporary Sanskrit anthologies, which survive from the twelfth century onwards. As the original version of the *Sattasaī* is irretrievable, we have made a selection from the 964 poems of Weber's edition and have ordered the poems in sections according to topic, following our own judgment and interpretation and adding an introduction to each section. In our translations of the poems we have followed the text as reconstructed by Weber. The few instances where we have preferred a variant reading to that adopted by Weber are indicated in an appendix.

Many of the poems, as we have noted, are in the form of conversations or monologues, and in translating them we have been concerned to make verbal register and tone fit the intention of the speaker. She (for in most cases the speaker is a woman) may want to pass on a message meant for her lover's ears alone, she may be desperate, annoyed or in the grip of anger, she may give vent to her frustration or she may be just pathetic. These intentions and emotions have to be brought out subtly but no less clearly, as the point of a poem may hinge on the fact of the girl's being naive or jealous or pathetic.

The style of the original poems varies considerably. Side by side with utterances consisting of a quick stream of short, crisp sentences there are poems with long, slow compounds. Some poems have dense patterns of assonance and a heavily figurative language; others are made up of straightforward, unadorned statements. We have tried to convey the varying tone of the originals. But sometimes the style of the original poem is altered in translation. A case in point is poem 614, which opens with two long compounds:

paḍhamaṇilīṇamahuramahu-
 lohillāliulavaddhajhaṃkāraṃ
ahimaarakiraṇaṇiuruṃ-
 vacuṃviaṃ dalaï kamalavaṇaṃ

Bees settle on it,
Buzzing wildly,
Lusting for its sweet nectar
But the lotus opens
Only after being kissed by the sun.

If the translation is relatively short and simple, this is because the poem features several convoluted circumlocutions, such as the nouns *ula* "group" in *āliula* and *ṇiuruṃva* "cluster" in *ahi-maarakiraṇaṇiuruṃva* to express the plural, and the word *ahi-maara* "which creates (-*ara*) non-coldness (*a-hima*)" for "the sun." This choice of words seems to have been largely determined by the desire to create sound effects (*lohillāliulavaddha* and *ahimaarakiraṇaṇiurumva*), which we have tried partially to reproduce.

The conversational flavor of the poems is underlined by the frequent use of vocatives in addressing friends and relatives as well as in expressing scorn ("You dimwit," "You fool"). Occasionally the vocative seems to be part of a kind of literary game, as in poem 207, where the first three feet are in the form of vocatives:

> Your long hair sways like a peacock's fan,
> Your thighs quiver, your eyes half close,
> With long pauses you sort of play the man.
> Now do you see what hard work it is
> For a man?

The poems may also differ in the use of figurative language. Some poems are simply a series of similes, like the following, in which the speaker ecstatically produces one comparison after another for a girl's hair:

> The girl's thick, fragrant hair
> Is like a column of smoke rising from the fire of love,
> Like a bunch of peacock's tail-feathers
> Waved by the conjuror to distract his audience,
> Like the victory banner of youth. [650]

But the simile also features in elaborate puns. In the following poem a woman's breasts are compared to a good poem, and each word describing the breasts applies simultaneously to the object of comparison, the poem:

> Who is not captivated by a woman's breasts,
>   That, like a good poem,
>   Are a pleasure to grasp,
>   Are weighty, compressed, and nicely ornamented? [651]

In the *Sattasaī* puns like these are rare, certainly when one compares later poetry in Sanskrit, where they were considered the acme of poetic skill. Only a few such poems from the *Sattasaī* have been translated here, as in most cases two translations would have been required and the whole point lost. The alternative was to write lengthy explanatory notes in addition to the introductions to the individual sections. But one of our principles of selection has been to omit any poem that required annotation to make it comprehensible.

Weber, the editor of the *Sattasaī*, was the first person to translate the poems (into German), but his versions remain buried in the learned publications in which they first appeared. Mention should be made of the translation into Italian by Giuliano Boccali, Daniela Sagramoso and Cinzia Pieruccini (1990), which is as judicious as it is elegant. Translations into English have so far been less felicitous: the only one to include all seven hundred verses of the so-called vulgate (corresponding to Weber (1881) nos. 1–700) is by Radhagovinda Basak (1970). Beside often missing or obscuring the point of the poems, it is too literal and unidiomatic to give any idea of the quality of the original. Considering that the *Sattasaī* is not only the earliest anthology of lyric verse from India but also arguably the most interesting, this relative neglect is astounding.

INVITATION

1

Among countless elegant poems,
King Hāla, patron of poets,
Has selected seven hundred.   [3]

2

Shame on those who cannot appreciate
This ambrosial Prakrit poetry
But pore instead
Over treatises on love.   [2]

3

Poems, songs, the sound of the lute,
And impudent women,
To men who have no taste for such things
They are a punishment.   [815]

EXCHANGING GLANCES

It is customary for parents to arrange marriages. Anxious for their daughter to be without reproach and untouched by gossip, they keep a close watch on her. Beyond a certain age boys and girls are more or less effectively segregated, with the result that they become all the more interested in each other. So we see the boy walking past the girl's house, trying to get a glimpse of her, and the girl peeping through the gaps in the fence at the boy walking by (4). The boy is shy of the girl's parents, while she tries to conceal from them her interest in the boy. Either she shows no emotion when the boy walks past (21), or she looks at everyone with equal affection so that her parents notice no difference (22). The girls' coquettish glances are often too subtle for the slightly oafish village boys, who require something cruder and more explicit. This is the particular fate of the village headman's daughter, whose father is a member of the village elite (19).

A number of poems deal with the village boys' fascination with breasts. For example, they hang around the woman florist, who raises her arms to show off her wares (9). The girls, knowing the boys' interest, do not hesitate to give them a glimpse of their breasts (7).

The occasional festival brings a welcome change. Holī is even now notorious for the licence it offers young lovers. During this festival high-caste and low-caste, master and servant, boy and girl throw colored powder at each other. At last girls get a chance to attract the attention of the boys they fancy. In one poem, however, the girl is so excited that the powder turns to paste and remains glued to her sweaty hands (35). In another poem the girl, anxious to remove all trace of the red powder from her hands, goes on feverishly washing them until someone reminds her that pink is the natural color of her palms (36). Another occasion for lovers to exchange more than glances is the village fire, when buckets of water are passed from hand to hand (40). More often, in a crowd, all the boy and girl can do is look at each other (31).

How desperate a boy or girl can be to establish some form of contact is seen in the poem where the girl bathes in the river in which the boy has previously washed himself with some kind of stinging soap, thereby ruining her soft skin (42). A counterpart is the poem describing a young man downriver, who drinks the soapy water of the girl upstream (43). Riverbanks in the part of India described here are generally quite steep. One way for a girl to attract a boy's attention and even to touch him is to take the most difficult path possible, so that he is forced to come and help her (44). Another sly girl leaps out of the way of some mud, landing as if by accident on the boy's foot (45).

If all this creates a taste for more, then the lovers will have to be more daring. It is not enough for the girl to take a few steps out of the house (47), and the boy should take greater risks than just circling around the girl's house (48).

4

Like a bird in a cage
Moving from one gap to the next,
With trembling eye
She peeps through the fence
As you walk past.   [220]

5

What is she to do
If, wobbling on tiptoe
And squeezing her breasts against the fence,
She still can't see you?   [221]

6

With its leaves pushing through
The gaps in the fence
The castor oil plant seems to be telling
The youths of the village
"Here lives a farmer's wife
With breasts this big." [257]

7

The girl has left open her dark blue bodice,
Like a door two inches ajar,
To show the young men
A sample of her breasts. [622]

8

Eager to feast his eyes
On the flower seller's
Gorgeous shoulders,
The young rake finds an excuse
For hanging around
By cross-questioning her
About her prices. [599]

9

Lifting up her lovely arms
To display the freshly plucked flowers,
The garland seller plucks at
The hearts of young men. [597]

10

With those damned breasts
Like the two bumps on a young elephant's forehead,

Firm, full and prominent, pressing against each other,
She can hardly breathe
Let alone move. [258]

11

It takes two feet to support the woman's broad hips.
So how can her waist on its own
Support her heavy breasts? [803]

12

Why do you groan as you carry them
—Two heaps piled with your rivals' jealousy,
Two vessels brimful of beauty,
Two elephant lobes stuffed with love?
In their hearts men by the hundred
Are sharing the burden
Of your breasts. [260]

13

Her round breast
Bulging out of a dark blue blouse
Looks like the moon
Peering from behind a cloud
Heavy with rain. [395]

14

The girl's breasts
Are like golden pots filled with the jewels of affection.
In the middle of each
King Love has set his dark seal. [813]

15

Due to these cursed villagers
Who brandish a cudgel at a mere pinprick

I dare not set eyes on my lover
Though we live in the same village.   [502]

16

Aunt,
If these sanctimonious people object,
Let them.
One can't help it if one's eyes stray
Toward the headman's son.   [610]

17

We should not be seen talking
Because people disapprove.
But how can one help setting eyes
Even on a person one detests
If he happens to cross one's path?   [515]

18

Not caring what people might say
And pushing her parents aside,
The poor girl
With no hope of ever seeing you again,
Lay rolling on the ground crying her heart out.   [484]

19

You dimwit,
What do you mean she didn't say anything to you?
This village headman's daughter,
Who in front of her elders looked at you
With half-closed eyes and face slightly averted,
Without blinking once.   [370]

20

You fool,
How can you say she didn't say a word?

She looked at you all the time
But her sight was blurred
By the tears welling up in her eyes.   [371]

21

In front of her parents
She showed no emotion
When you passed by,
But a tear that clung to her lashes
Fell when she closed her eyes.   [367]

22

The way she looks at you,
With love and affection written all over her face,
She looks at everyone else as well,
To conceal her feelings.   [199]

23

To watch you
As you walked away
She twisted round so far
The tears could be seen
Streaming down her back.   [223]

24

When she could no longer follow you
With her eyes stretching almost to her ears
She poured a libation with rolling tears
To the past pleasure of seeing you.   [338]

25

Don't peep at him on the sly.
Look him straight in the eye.

That way you'll get a good look at him
And people will take you for an innocent. [225]

26

This girl is so shy
That the feelings aroused in her
By the sight of you,
Like a poor man's dreams, find
Fulfillment only in the mind. [612]

27

Aunt,
A glimpse of that man,
Whom one could never tire of staring at,
Is like drinking water in a dream:
It has not quenched my thirst. [93]

28

Wretched shyness stops her every limb
From acting naturally,
But even with her parents standing by
It cannot force her not to use her ears. [618]

29

As he walks towards me, passes,
And then looks back,
My lover's tremulous glances
Are to me like Love's arrows
Whatever they may be to others. [210]

30

Why, my hips,
Have you not grown as wide as the street

So that I might touch that lovely man
As he tries to escape
The awkward scene with my parents?   [393]

31

In the midst of the crowd
A boy speaks through his eyes
Shining with delight,
And a girl replies
As her limbs break out in a sweat.   [341]

32

He looked at her
In such a way,
And she at him,
That, at the same moment,
They both consummated their love.   [627]

33

His eyes are glued to her face,
And she is intoxicated at the sight of him.
So utterly content are these two,
There might not be another man or woman on earth.   [498]

34

Have a care—
The poor girl, wearing a freshly dyed dress,
Is distributing festival cakes from door to door
In the hope of catching a glimpse of you.   [328]

35

Trembling and bouncing with excitement,
She holds a handful of colored powder

To throw at her lover,
But it has turned into perfumed water. [312]

36

Foolish girl,
Why are you still washing
The red powder from your soft palms
That are by nature pink
As a spray of coral? [680]

37

Why are you trying to wash away that powder
Which someone innocently threw at you
On the Holī festival?
It has already been washed away by the sweat
Streaming off the nipples of your round breasts. [369]

38

Young girl,
On this day of Holī
—Your breasts dusted with flour,
Your eyes red from too much liquor,
A lotus stuck in your hair
And mango shoots behind your ears—
You are a credit to our village. [826]

39

Look at her breasts
Powdered with the flour
She grinds for the festival,
Like two white geese sitting in the shade
Of the lotus of her face. [626]

40

Even though everything I had went up in flames
I am overjoyed,
For during the fire
It was he who took the bucket of water
From my hand into his.   [229]

41

That our village burnt down
As though there were no help for it,
Despite the number of young men at hand,
Is the doing of your wicked breasts
Which in the confusion
Were swaying about.   [714]

42

Haven't you heard how that lovely girl ruined her soft skin
By bathing in the Godā
Just where you had smeared yourself
With stinging rose-apple lotion?   [189]

43

Mother,
That young man
Who downriver drank the water
That was bitter with my turmeric soap,
Has as good as drunk my heart.   [246]

44

On the pretext that the steps
Down to the Godā were uneven,
She clung to his breast

While he, purely out of concern,
Held her in a tight embrace.   [193]

45

If that woman, who stepped on your foot
As she leapt away from the mud,
Were so indifferent,
Why, my dear, is your body now covered
With gooseflesh?   [67]

46

Though she ran out quickly
She failed to spot you.
In this damned village the street twists
Like a snake hit on the head.   [809]

47

At the sound of your voice
She rushed out of the house
In her desire to see you.
Once you had passed
She had to be carried back again.   [506]

48

Of course the sight of her precious face
Is enough to rob any man of his senses.
But to glimpse the outskirts of her village
Is a joy in itself.   [168]

LOVERS' MEETINGS

If lovers want to meet in secret an opportunity offers itself when the girl is working in the fields or when she has been sent out to pick flowers. Young girls are left on their own in the fields to chase away birds. But this job, and with it the chance to meet her lover, ends with the harvest: as the ripening rice begins to droop, so does the head of the apprehensive girl (66). It's the same story with flower picking: at a certain point the flowers bloom no more (64). And the bushes on the river bank, under which the lovers took cover, begin to drop their leaves (63). Another hindrance to lovers' secret meetings is the holy man who wanders around the countryside in search of deserted spots where he can rest or meditate (62).

Lovers who want to be absolutely certain of secrecy try to meet on a dark night in the rainy season (68). But to get to the assignation in absolute darkness is not easy. The girl has to practice at home by walking around with her eyes closed (69). Besides, the paths are muddy and slippery (71), and the girl has to wrap herself from head to toe in dark clothes so that no part of her body will show and betray her. When at last her lover sees her all muffled up, he shrinks from the task of unwrapping and wants to send her back (72). But there is no alternative: it is the only time of the year when the moon, hidden behind thick, dark rain clouds, cannot spoil a nighttime assignation (73).

The meeting is not always a success, either because the boy is a thickhead who does not know what to do or say (58, 60) or because he imagines that things happen of their own accord

(59). In other cases the girl is unable to find the exact place where they agreed to meet (54), or the boy does not show up or is late (53). Sometimes it is the girl who has left the boy waiting (79). With all these delays, the pleasure the lovers experience does not last long. Daybreak, whose coming they dread, ruthlessly signals its end (80).

Another complicating factor is the need to hide all traces of the night's escapade. Lack of sleep causes suspicion (81). On the other hand, if the girl looks just the same as she did the day before, her friends don't believe her when she tells them she had a meeting with her lover (82). Telltale signs such as nail scratches or teeth marks on the girl's body are in the end the only proofs of the lovers having met. These the girl protects with loving care (83).

49

When an opportunity finally offers itself,
Endlessly weighing the pros and cons
And considering the matter carefully,
As if one had all the time in the world,
Are sure ways to bungle one's chances.   [214]

50

Don't bother about your makeup, girl,
Just go to him quickly, while he wants you.
Once his longing is over
He won't give you a thought.   [21]

51

You won't make anyone happy
By sitting here
Removing with a bamboo needle
The traces of turmeric soap
From the meshes of your filigree bracelet.   [80]

52

When he comes what shall I do?
What shall I say?
And how will it be?
The girl's heart trembles
At her first chance to be reckless.   [187]

53

Listening for the rustle of dead leaves
Stirred by his footfall,
The wanton woman awaits her lover in the arbor.   [365]

54

Having missed the assignation
In all those reed beds,
She looks for you everywhere
As though in search of lost treasure.   [318]

55

Look!
The freshly dyed skirt
That the woman hurriedly kicked off
In her desire to make love
Hangs over the bower
Like a banner proclaiming her immodesty.   [461]

56

Embarrassed
By the girl losing her virginity,
A flock of birds
Flies up from the bushes by the river,
Seeming to say "Ah! Ah!" with their wings.   [218]

57

Lucky are they who live
In a mountain village
Where one can make love
Undisturbed
Beneath a leafy hedge
Or in deep thickets of reeds
That bend and sway in the wind.   [637]

58

Why waste your time with sweetwood flowers,
You silly?
Just pull the skirt from my hips.
Whom can I call to in this wood?
The village is a long way off
And I am all by myself.   [877]

59

Even an old cow gives milk
At the touch of an expert milker.
My son,
You'll have a hard time finding one
That gives milk
Merely at a glance.   [462]

60

I have heard so much about you from others
And now at last I see you with my own eyes.
Please, my dear, say something
So that my ears, too, may drink nectar.   [805]

61

My boy,
Why go picking flowers?

The gods are perfectly happy with offerings of water
And the banks of the Godāvarī
Are the ruin of many a young man.   [355]

62

Your holiness,
It's safe for you to walk in the village now.
The dog that bothered you
Has been killed by a fierce lion
Who lives in the thickets of the Godā.   [175]

63

O sweetwood tree,
Whose branches, bowed by the weight of blossom,
Reach to the ground
In the broad thickets on the bank of the Godā,
Do me a favor
And shed your leaves slowly.   [103]

64

Weeping,
The woman gathers the very last sweetwood flowers
Now painful to behold,
Like the bones of a relative
On the funeral pyre.   [104]

65

Cheer up!
Don't cry for the paddy turning white.
There's the field of hemp in bloom
Like a dancer with her face painted yellow!   [9]

66

Just like the rice,
Each day her head bends lower
And her face grows paler
—The girl who guards the paddy,
As she grows more fearful of the day
When her occupation will cease.   [693]

67

She does not answer when spoken to
And is cross with everyone
For no other reason
Than that the bush on the river bank is burning.   [416]

68

His unmanly bliss
And my unwomanly boldness
Are known only to the swollen waters of the Godā
And the midnights of the rainy season.   [231]

69

Because even on this dark night she intends to meet her lover,
The girl paces up and down indoors
With her eyes tightly shut.   [249]

70

Watch out!
The path is slippery after today's shower.
If you grope for the hand of your lover
Whom you imagine is standing beside you,
You are bound to fall over.   [766]

71

Even now I can see
The mud in that wretched village,
Which I squelched through on those dark nights
In the rainy season
Just to please you.
And what did I get out of it,
You shameless man?　[445]

72

That she has come all swathed in black
Shouldn't deter you.
Even a tight breast band
Is prized off in the heat of love.　[521]

73

How easy it is for the moon
To spoil my nightly assignations!
For there is no end to the cascade of moonbeams
With which it empties itself into the lake of the sky.　[491]

74

You will meet him,
No need to hurry,
Wait till the moon is full.
For no one will tell your face
Apart from moonlight
Any more than milk from milk.　[609]

75

Child, if your heart is set on secret passion,
Don't go out in the dark,

For the darker it is
The more clearly visible you will be,
Like the flame of a lamp.   [415]

76

The messenger is late,
The moon is high,
And the night is passing.
Everything's awry
But to whom can I complain?   [854]

77

Thinking that you would come,
The wakeful first part of the night went by in a minute.
The remainder of the night,
Filled with disappointment,
Seemed to last a year.   [385]

78

The moon was bright,
My moon-faced beauty,
And the night was long,
My long-eyed girl.
The four watches passed.
Though, with you away,
They seemed to last
A hundred.   [252]

79

Dearest,
I know you are not really asleep,
Just keeping your eyes closed.
I can see goose pimples rising as I kiss your cheek.
I won't be late again.   [20]

80

Every one knows the hardhearted lover
Leaves at dawn.
Venerable Night, stretch on
So that morning will not come.   [46]

81

If you are not his lover,
How come you sleep every day,
Your limbs as weak
As those of a newborn buffalo calf,
Drunk on its mother's milk?   [65]

82

You look just as you did yesterday,
So you must be bragging.
In fact you did not see him,
For if you had,
You would no longer look so well.   [478]

83

The poor girl cherishes the teeth marks
You have just left on her cheeks
Like a pledge,
Protecting them with a fence of gooseflesh.   [96]

WRONG CHOICES AND DISAPPOINTMENTS

To meet her lover the girl has taken considerable risks. It is all the more painful to discover that he is not what at first sight he seemed to be. When no longer so keen to see her, he pleads fear of gossip as his excuse (96). He can be fickle and unreliable (110), and the more attractive he is, the more difficult she finds it to keep him for herself (113, 114). It is not long before the girl realizes she has chosen the wrong man. In one poem (98) she is compared to a pumpkin that has climbed over a trellis designed for less heavy plants.

The boy may suffer similar setbacks. He may choose a woman who has proven unapproachable even for much more experienced men (100), or he undertakes an affair much too light-heartedly, but when he asks for his heart back is told that that is not the way things work (103). He is also compared to a young calf excitedly following his fancies and is advised to grow up and become as sober as a bull (104).

The unhappy girl blames her heart for judging merely by appearances and following its own feelings (105). Her unhappiness begins to show: she cries, sighs and wastes away. But what can she do about it? It is all in the hands of fate (123, 125). Her situation is worse than if her lover were absent abroad. For in that case she could at least hope for his return (126). Sometimes love simply evaporates for no obvious reason (122).

84

If you want to be happy
Take care in choosing a lover,
For what is dear to you
Does not bring happiness
Unless you are dear to it.   [652]

85

All the worthy people I meet,
All the generous and discerning ones
Already receive your favors,
You clever devil,
Poverty.   [673]

86

Are these the pleasures
For which I threw myself upon you,
Brushing aside the warnings of my friends,
And for lack of which my life
Now hangs in the balance?   [158]

87

Dear friend,
The man for whom I abandoned modesty,
Destroyed my character
And lost my good name
Now treats me just like anyone else.   [525]

88

Don't trust those bastards!
They're just like dogs:
First they fawn

But once they've had their way
They turn their backs on you. [688]

89

First you made her waste away,
Then taught her how to weep and wail,
Then made her flout all decency.
So, please, do not neglect her now. [348]

90

The poor thing is a decent girl
Yet in one day, you sinner,
You have taught her to languish,
To yawn and to weep. [352]

91

The tear in the eye of the wretched girl,
Betraying thoughts of her beloved,
Wells up, brims over and flows out
Like a flood of grief. [377]

92

When we asked her whom she was thinking of
She replied: "No one,"
And began to cry so piteously
That we cried with her. [389]

93

You fool,
When I asked what had really happened
The girl's reply brought tears to my eyes:
The way she joked and swore
That there was nothing to tell. [357]

94

Even to someone who knows nothing about it
She tells who it is who has broken her bracelets.
Either the poor girl is naïve
Or she really loves the man who has made her so
    unhappy. [438]

95

Nowadays people restrain me
But when this love,
Which like a poison courses through all my limbs,
First began
They were mute. [699]

96

Never mind the gossip:
Judge by your own feelings.
Anyway,
You have grown so cool
That you are beyond reproach. [201]

97

Friend, this is just the way things happen—
Stop your tears, don't turn your face away—
Like the tendrils of a young cucumber,
One's affections twine around an object
That does not stay. [10]

98

You little pumpkin,
The way you climb over another plant's trellis,
Abandoning the one designed to bear your weight

—One of these days, I tell you,
You will fall and burst open. [768]

99

Heart,
After getting stuck here and there,
Like a log
Borne along by the current of a shallow stream,
One day you will be fuel for someone. [105]

100

My son,
Don't try to climb this trumpetflower tree:
It has no branches to hold on to.
Name me a man who did not fall
When trying to climb this wretched tree. [468]

101

Foolish heart,
Why so distressed?
Worse will befall you,
Running after a man
In thrall to another. [510]

102

You rush ahead, following your own fancy,
Always in quest of the unattainable man.
One day, heart, as you roam the skies,
You'll crash. [202]

103

My boy,
Don't be so hasty.

This isn't the place
To leave things for safekeeping.
As far as I know,
Hearts deposited here
Are not returned.   [154]

104

Young calf,
Blushing red as a tender mango shoot,
Running with ears pricked
Towards the house of your desire,
Assume the cool whiteness of a bull!   [19]

105

Heart,
Please, enough of this!
How can you slight us and attach yourself
To someone whose real worth is unknown,
Judging merely by your own feelings?   [345]

106

To fall in love with a man who returns your love,
One who is full of kindness and affection,
Makes sense.
But to give one's heart to a man who is utterly heartless
Is laughable.   [41]

107

Though he may for a moment
Slip one's mind
One still remembers a person.
But love,
Once it is but a memory,

Vanishes
For it is something immaterial.   [95]

108

My son,
Only someone who has acquired merit
In past lives
Can win the love
Of women
With their sly look, sly talk,
Sly smile and sly walk.   [174]

109

A man so handsome
One cannot tire of looking at him,
Who shares one's troubles as well as one's joys,
Proves faithful and returns one's love
—Such a man is only to be got through merit
Accumulated over many lives.   [99]

110

He can be captured only with the greatest difficulty
And once captured he is difficult to keep,
And even if captured,
He is not captured
Unless his heart is captured as well.   [305]

111

Not so long ago your eyes were glued to my cheeks,
They could not look away.
I am still the same as then,
So are the cheeks,
Not so your eyes.   [939]

112

Fate,
Please, don't let me be born as a human again.
But if it must be,
Then don't let me fall in love.
But if it must be,
Then don't let me fall in love
With a man who is so hard to get. [844]

113

How can a woman
Who for five whole days
Has been the lover of such an attractive man
Ask for one day more?
One cannot feast on dainties. [72]

114

There is pleasure,
There is delight,
And there is no cause for regret
As long as one does not fall in love
With a man popular with women.
For such a man is one big storehouse of trouble. [931]

115

Since love is fickle
I dance to my lover's tune.
A creeper twines itself
Around the unbending tree. [304]

116

She wept as long as she had tears to weep,
She grew as thin as her body would allow,

And, poor thing,
Sighed as long as she had breath to sigh. [141]

117

I suppose you have never felt
The pain of grief,
That you ask me, laughingly,
Why I am so thin.
When you have found a fickle lover yourself,
I will explain. [157]

118

She cherishes her heart
Because you live in it,
Her eyes
Because with them she can gaze at you,
Even her body
Because it grows thin in your absence. [40]

119

My heart is lodged in your heart,
My eyes, like eyes in a painting,
Are immovably fixed on your face,
It is only my body
That is wasting away
For lack of your embrace. [485]

120

Why cry, why lament,
Why, slender girl,
Get angry with each and every one?
Love is a lethal poison.
And, tell me,
Can anyone withstand it? [517]

121

Silly boy,
However close the ties of affection,
If people don't see one another,
Love gradually seeps away
Just like water between one's cupped hands.   [236]

122

Love vanishes
Through not seeing enough of one another,
Through seeing too much of one another,
Through spiteful gossip,
And sometimes just like that.   [81]

123

His image is in my eyes,
His touch on my limbs,
His words in my ear
And his heart in my heart.
To separate us needs more than just fate.   [132]

124

Aunt,
It pains me now to realize
How fragile a thing love is,
Like treasure beheld in a dream
That vanishes in the light of day.   [423]

125

Whatever the mind
With the pen of hope
Writes on the tablet of the heart

Fate, like a naughty child,
Wipes out with a secret smile.   [658]

126

Hope helps one bear
The burning fire of separation
From the man one loves.
But, mother, when the man one loves
Lives in the same village yet keeps away,
That is worse than death.   [43]

THE GO-BETWEEN

After the first meeting with her lover the girl is anxious to know what is going to happen next. Contact between the lovers is maintained with the help of a go-between, who is usually a close friend and confidante of the girl. She despatches this messenger with precise and elaborate instructions and awaits her return with impatience. Normally the go-between carries out her instructions to the letter, but in some cases she may have such a low opinion of the boy that she refuses to pass on the message entrusted to her by the girl. According to her, he is such an untrustworthy fellow that the girl is better off dead (134, 135). One complication is that the go-between is herself a young girl and not insensitive to the charms of the lover. In poem 138 she returns with a bruised lip, not from mere talking it would seem.

127

Sweating all over
From just mentioning her lover's name,
She was so busy instructing the messenger
That she did not notice
They had arrived in front of his house.   [440]

128

Over and over again
I told her the words you confided to me,

But claiming she hadn't quite caught them
She made me repeat the message a hundred times.   [198]

129

What he wanted me to say to you
I didn't catch
Because he stammered so much
And sighed such burning sighs.   [859]

130

"He's not coming,"
Teased the go-between.
But look:
Despite her feigning,
A thrill of excitement
Steals over her face.   [856]

131

She will go to his house,
Then wait her chance,
Then approach him,
Then say what she has to say.
But what will she get for reply?   [918]

132

Go-between! You're brilliant
—The way you know how to mix rough with smooth.
Please, do it in such a way
That he itches all over
Without having a rash.   [181]

133

"I have grown thin in your absence."
"The fire of separation is hard to bear."

"My life hangs in the balance."
Why am I telling you this, my friend?
You know yourself the sort of thing that needs saying. [486]

134

I am not her go-between,
You are not her lover,
So what have we to do with each other?
But let me tell you the truth:
She is dying,
And the disgrace is yours. [178]

135

Wait a moment, my handsome friend,
I've a message from someone.
Or perhaps I haven't.
She always acts so rashly,
She'd be better off dead.
No, I've nothing to tell you. [604]

136

This wretched body is the ruin of me:
In daily humiliation
It totters from door to door
On other people's business
Yet refuses to die. [134]

137

Addressing my lover again and again.
Dear friend, all this trouble for my sake.
What you do
You seem to do out of true love. [860]

138

If he does not do what you ask him
On my behalf, you useless messenger,
Why not give your lips a rest?
They are already bruised.   [718]

139

You always say: "Your business is my business,"
But today, dear go-between,
You've taken it all too literally
And gone too far.   [861]

THE YOUNG COUPLE

A girl's husband is usually chosen by her parents—a choice that rarely coincides with her own (140). At this stage many names are dropped either to test or to tease her (143).

The girl is expected to be completely without experience in matters of love. To her husband her ingenuousness is a special attraction (146). At the same time her shyness, when he tries to talk to her, makes him feel like a criminal (147). She is so frightened of everything to do with sex that she wraps her skirt twice around her hips (148) or holds it between her thighs, which she keeps tightly pressed together (149).

It is up to the husband to initiate his new wife into the secrets of love (153). Sometimes he finds he is dealing with a girl who has already picked up quite a bit of know-how before getting married (155). Should he not realize this, he makes a complete fool of himself by his overcautious approach (152).

The young wife not only lacks experience in lovemaking but is also inexpert in the kitchen, not knowing how to keep the fire alight, making a lot of smoke, and being frightened by the flames. To her husband, though, her soot-smeared face is a source of joy (173).

Ideally, and certainly in the early days of their marriage, the couple cannot get enough of each other: they have eyes for no one else. They find even a short separation hard to bear. Two poems (170, 171) describe how the husband pays an unexpected visit to his young wife, who is staying with her parents. His passion is redoubled when he hears the tinkle of her bracelets in the backyard of the house, and she too tries but fails to stifle her feelings in her parents' presence.

140

Aunt,
Marry the girl to the person she fancies.
Can't you see she is pining away?
"'Person I fancy'? What do you mean?"
So saying the girl fell in a faint. [298]

141

She stares into thin air,
Heaves long sighs,
Smiles vacantly
And mutters nonsense:
There must be something on her mind. [296]

142

If he is not dear to you
How comes it, my friend,
That at the mere mention of his name
Your face opens like a lotus
Touched by the rays of the sun? [343]

143

He seems to be
The beginning, middle and end
Of every conversation.
Am I to suppose, dear aunt,
That in this entire village
There is only one young man? [650]

144

Aunt!
There goes the young man

Whom all the hussies in turn
Try to grab hold of,
Just like the water in the only well in the village
On a hot summer's day.   [294]

145

Look,
When the women start singing the wedding songs
Goose pimples break out on the bride-to-be
As if they too want to hear
The bridegroom's name.   [644]

146

She does not look at you,
Does not allow you to touch her face,
Says nothing.
Yet,
In some mysterious way,
Being with a young bride is pure joy.   [647]

147

When he asks her a question
She does not reply,
When he touches her
She recoils,
When he kisses her
She starts to cry,
And when he attempts an embrace
His young wife's silence
Makes him feel like a criminal.   [649]

148

When her husband told her to come to bed
She looked away

And, with an embarrassed laugh,
Wrapped her skirt twice around her thighs.   [504]

149

Feigning sleep
The husband turned over
And let a trembling hand fall as if by accident
On the knot of his young wife's skirt
Which she held firmly between her thighs.   [648]

150

The satisfaction of that first night
Was nothing compared to seeing the embarrassment
Next day
On the lotus of her face.   [209]

151

I refuse to believe that she who,
Cheeks flushed with excitement,
Is so demanding while making love
Can really suit him,
However meek she may be next morning.   [23]

152

Friend,
I had to laugh
When his hand fumbled at my thin skirt,
Which stuck tight to my sweating thighs.   [723]

153

I love you,
Of that I am certain.

What I do not know
And what you must teach me, please,
Is how you will come to love me.   [750]

154

I long to be dear to you
But do not know how.
Teach me yourself
How to be loved.   [948]

155

How old is she,
This damned girl?
And when did she learn it all?
She already knows everything
That a mature woman knows.   [825]

156

When her relatives whirled around the sheet
Said to be stained with the young bride's blood
The virgin's lover looked on with a glint in his eye.   [457]

157

I suspect the reed beds by the river
As well as the young men
Had a good laugh when they heard
The solemn song of blessing
On the eve of my wedding.   [645]

158

He was embarrassed
But I laughed and gave him a hug

When he groped for the knot
Of my skirt and found it
Already undone.   [351]

159

It was like a miracle,
Like finding treasure,
Like being king in heaven,
Like a draught of nectar,
That one moment
When I saw her undressed.   [125]

160

How can I describe her?
Once you see her body
You cannot take your eyes off it:
They are like a helpless cow
Stuck in the mud.   [271]

161

On whichever part of her body
One's eye falls first
There it stays.
No one has ever seen the whole of her body.   [234]

162

Whatever part of my body he stares at
I cover.
At the same time I want him to see it.   [73]

163

The moment I see him
I will cover my eyes with both hands,

But how am I going to hide my body
Which is bristling like a spiky *kadamba* blossom?   [314]

164

When one sees him
He gives satisfaction to the eyes,
When one thinks of him
He gives satisfaction to the mind,
When he speaks
He gives satisfaction to the ears:
Dear mother-in-law,
My husband is always delightful.   [653]

165

Going over everything you do,
Everything you say,
Every trick of your eyes
—One day is too short.   [378]

166

The things we say
That are commonplace,
When he says them,
Fill the heart with joy.   [651]

167

Away from me
She is like deadly poison,
Together again
She is sweeter than nectar.
How did the Creator manage
To combine these two potions
In my darling?   [235]

168

Some lucky women are able to prance around
With sighs and shivers and raptures.
But when women like us see their husbands
They completely forget themselves. [361]

169

My dear,
Only women who do not see you
Stay happy:
They sleep properly,
Hear what is said to them,
And do not muddle their words. [418]

170

The tinkle of bracelets
As she took a bath in the backyard of her parents' house
Redoubled the passion of her husband
Who had arrived in the late afternoon. [685]

171

Surprised by her husband's arrival
At her parents' house,
The girl was annoyed with her bracelets
For dancing up and down her arms
And threatening to slip off. [822]

172

The mynah bird has prattled
In front of the elders
About what we get up to in bed
So that, for the moment,
I don't know which way to turn. [590]

173

The husband laughed at his wife's face
Which, smudged with soot
That stuck to her hand from kitchen work,
Looked more than ever like the moon. [14]

174

Don't get annoyed:
There's nothing wrong with your cooking.
That the fire won't burn but only smokes
Is because it wants to inhale your breath
That has the fragrance of red trumpetflowers. [13]

175

Dear girl,
The flames reflected on your cheeks
When you kindle the kitchen fire
Resemble blossoming twigs
Hanging down from your ears. [733]

176

You silly girl,
Why do you shrink away each time you blow into the fire?
These flames reflected on your round breasts
Flicker but will not touch you. [732]

177

Hey there, daughter—
Keep on whitewashing that wall.
Don't stop because you think the job's already done.
Can't you see? It's the moonlight of your face
That makes it look so white. [747]

MAKING LOVE

Love play begins with embracing and kissing (178), the girl's lips tasting of wine (184). Stealing a kiss is a pleasure in itself, though it may involve a struggle (187). Or it happens almost by accident, as when the man is asked to blow pollen out of the woman's eye (188).

Often man and wife prove incompatible: he may like variety, which she cannot provide (200, 201). But if she spices things up, he is likely to wonder who taught her how (199). One of the more exciting variations is when the woman sits on top of the man. The god of love is then said to take aim from behind her (209). The woman needs strong thighs to make love in this way, especially when she happens to be pregnant (205). In one poem (208) the woman in this squatting position is compared to a *vidyādharī*, a celestial being who in Indian art is depicted as flying through the air in a squatting position.

In the indigenous treatises on law and custom it is expressly forbidden to make love to a woman during her period. The underlying belief is that the menstrual blood, which is considered a kind of female semen, increases the chances of getting a daughter. This prohibition, by its very existence, adds excitement to lovemaking at this time. Several poems refer to a practice, otherwise unknown, of women in their period smearing their faces with a mixture of clarified butter (*ghee*) and a red dye. As a result man and wife have to kiss very carefully to avoid smears on the man's face (215). At the same time such smears show that he is so infatuated with his wife that he is prepared to flout convention. When, the morning after, a man's elder wives see traces of red from the younger wife's face on his shoulders, they know they have been superseded (217). In another poem (218) we see how a young, inexperienced wife has naively painted her face red in an attempt to stave off her husband's attentions and, in the event of this failing to deter him, she has also wrapped her skirt twice round her thighs.

Another custom mentioned is that of the man beating his wife with a twig by way of foreplay. This seems to be a practice popular among farmers, whose courting habits are considered to lack subtlety (189).

In the act of making love the intensity of desire is increased by biting and scratching. The traces left by nails and teeth are the measure of a man's infatuation, and consequently the wife had better not expose them unless she wants to make a laughingstock of her servile husband (222). At the same time scratches and tooth marks serve to reassure a mother, whose interest is in grandchildren and the continuation of the family line (221). In one poem the young wife mistakes the scratches on her breast for a safflower and tries in vain to brush it off (231). In the next (232) the woman, while inspecting her body for nail marks, unwittingly imprints pink traces on her breasts, as her eyes, which by literary convention resemble lotus petals, are mirrored in their polished expanse.

178

O auntie!
Hurrah for the embrace
That, like a violent wind, bends the tree of pride,
Gives pleasure to the whole body,
And is the prologue to the play of love.   [344]

179

Sandal paste does not work as well
As the wild delight of a tight embrace,
Which, even on the hottest summer day,
Succeeds in allaying a couple's fever.   [288]

180

With great difficulty
He released himself from my arms
As if untangling a tight knot
And I extracted my breasts
Deeply buried in his chest. [276]

181

By their wide and staring eyes
And the gooseflesh on their cheeks
These women betray their lovers
Who, hidden underwater,
Have put their arms around them. [559]

182

In the act of embracing their lovers
Young ladies toss the pearl necklaces
From their round breasts.
Even the praiseworthy
Sometimes get treated with disrespect. [429]

183

Finding no way between her full, upcurving breasts,
Her necklace of pearls dances upon her chest
Like the bubbles of foam on the Yamunā. [671]

184

Loose-hanging hair
To take in one's hands
And a mouth smelling of wine:
That's all young women need
To bring with them
As allurement in love. [545]

185

Her face is round like the moon,
Her lips taste like nectar,
Grabbing her by the hair
And giving her a passionate kiss,
What is that like?   [213]

186

I will never forget how she shook her head
When I tried to kiss her lips
And her tresses flew in all directions.
Her face looked like a lotus
Surrounded by a swarm of bees
Excited by its fragrance.   [78]

187

One time you get them only after a long search,
At another you kiss them after a struggle,
At yet another they are freely offered
—One pair of lover's lips
Is an inexhaustible source of delights.   [827]

188

When the wind has blown pollen
From the lotus on my ear
Into my eye
Only a god can steal a kiss
While blowing it out.   [176]

189

What the young farmer's wife only does
After being threatened with a twig

Every young maiden
In every household
Would love to be taught.   [862]

190

As soon as you have a supple twig in your hand
She runs across your path,
Hovers on either side of you,
And happens to be
Wherever you are looking.
You blockhead,
Can't you see the poor girl
Desperately wants a good thrashing?   [456]

191

At whichever part of her body
Her husband's younger brother
Aims the tender twig
Gooseflesh raises a palisade of sticks.   [28]

192

Thanks to you, prickly safflower tree,
Young girls will learn to suck in their breath,
To moan,
To twitch,
To flutter their hands
And make their bracelets rattle.   [392]

193

The lamp blown out,
Stifled sighs,
Fearful whispers,
Lips sealed by hundreds of vows:
Oh! the joys of stolen love.   [333]

194

Tell me,
Would you not get angry
When bothered at the wrong time and place?
What mother does not curse her little son, dear as he is,
If he comes crying while she is busy making love?   [400]

195

The pleasure of riding your thighs
Is for special people only.
Take the golden girdle:
It had to go through the ordeal of fire and water first.   [211]

196

Making love
With great sophistication,
For all the pleasure
Of constantly renewed passion,
Is not as rapturous
As making love
Wherever and however
With true affection.   [274]

197

In lovemaking, with its manifold and intricate delights,
Who is there to instruct women?
One can learn anything
Simply by being shown some affection.   [477]

198

That froward cow,
Which did not even wet the cowherd's hand

However much he squeezed her teats—
Look how she's now yielding milk
By the pail. [639]

199

Straightforward pleasure doesn't satisfy him, he says,
And if I spice it up,
He wonders who taught me that.
As I always get it wrong
How will I ever make him happy? [476]

200

My dear,
I am a simple person,
While my lover only likes fancy tricks.
Tell me, is there some other way of wiping my eyes? [666]

201

I am shy
And he is ready for anything,
But my friends will help me out,
So why should I paint my feet? [127]

202

If you are the scholar
You say you are,
Then go to her
And stop bothering us,
For she knows all the tricks in the book. [759]

203

Praise be to the fond attentions of prostitutes
Who minister to everyone's need for the pleasures of love
With a whole armory of wiles. [156]

204

You who like to make love upside down,
How can you ask if I am pregnant?
Is there a single drop of water left
In a jug turned upside down?   [656]

205

Our daughter-in-law is not so much distressed
By the very heavy weight in her womb
As by the fact that due to it
She can no longer make love
On top of her husband.   [483]

206

Let her play bunny hops.
Don't stop her.
She needs the training
So that later
When she sits on top of her husband
She does not collapse
Under the weight of her own thighs.   [196]

207

Your long hair sways like a peacock's fan,
Your thighs quiver, your eyes half close,
With long pauses you sort of play the man.
Now do you see what hard work it is
For a man?   [52]

208

The girl on top of her lover,
Her hair hanging loose,

Her earrings swinging
And her pearl necklace hovering,
Looks just like a *vidyādharī*
Who is about to fly away. [446]

209

The God of Love strings his bow
When women sit astride their husbands,
Thighs twitching,
Eyes closing
And hair tossing around. [616]

210

With fingertips clutching the river bank,
And hips gently moving with the waves,
The female frog,
Hanging over her mirror image in the water,
Looks like a woman making love
On top of her husband. [391]

211

Though people condemn it,
Though it is highly inauspicious
And considered most improper,
The sight of a woman during her period
Fills the heart with heavenly bliss. [480]

212

"People will be angry."
Let them be.
"They will disapprove."
Who cares?
Come, forget about your period

And snuggle down beside me,
For I can get no sleep. [530]

213

"Fool, don't you see I'm having my period.
Don't touch me
If you value your life."
I am ready to die right away,
Deer-eyed woman,
So why waste time? [950]

214

If you do not want to touch a woman during her period,
Why get in my way when you shouldn't?
I will touch you with my itchy hands
As I push past you. [481]

215

I will never forget how,
When her face was smeared with red ghee,
We kissed,
Carefully pouting our lips
So that our noses and foreheads
Wouldn't meet. [22]

216

The man who kissed me with such extraordinary care
When my face was smeared with red ghee
Now hardly cares even to touch me
Despite my wearing this lovely jewelry. [520]

217

His other wives shed large tears
As they see smears of red grease

From the youngest wife's face
On the husband's shoulder. [529]

218

When he asked his young wife
Why her face was still smeared with ghee,
She looked away in embarrassment
But smiled,
Her skirt wrapped twice around her thighs. [289]

219

I will never forget how my beloved ran off
In anger,
With red cheeks,
Stammering with trembling lips
That I should leave her alone. [192]

220

Once in a month
The God of Love, fully armed,
Resides in women whose clothes are stained,
Whose hair is tied in ugly braids,
And whose cheeks are pallid. [949]

221

When the wind tossed up the wife's skirt,
Exposing the tooth marks on her thighs,
Her mother was thrilled,
As if she had hit upon the lid of a pot of gold. [508]

222

The wind is tossing up your skirt.
Hide the tooth marks on your thighs,

You stupid girl,
Don't make a laughingstock
Of your doting husband.   [607]

223

You simpleton,
Shouldn't you be a little more discreet
When people ask how your lover behaves?
With all its leaves so fragrant,
What need has the marjoram for a mass of blooms?   [679]

224

Why so proud
About your husband having painted a pattern
On your breasts?
My husband would have done the same
If his hand had not trembled so much.   [830]

225

She walks about quite smoothly
So why pull a face at every step?
It must be her girdle
Chafing against the nail marks on her hip.   [463]

226

Pretending to smear on a salve,
The young girl with delicate fingers
Applies a white bandage to her wounded lip.   [458]

227

One breast oozes milk,
The other is covered with nail marks and gooseflesh:

Behold the housewife sitting between husband and
　son. [409]

228

"Take it and have a look!"
With a broad smile on her face
She hands her husband the jujube fruit
With the marks on it
Of their son's first pair of teeth. [200]

229

If one loves a man
He gives pleasure even while causing pain.
Though wounded by a lover's nails
Breasts thrill with gooseflesh. [100]

230

The waning moon veiled by the red sky at dawn
Looks like the nail mark on the young bride's bosom
Showing through her crimson gauze. [570]

231

Her friends told the young wife
That a safflower was clinging to her breast,
And burst into laughter
When she tried to brush off the nail marks. [145]

232

The young wife inspecting her heavy and prominent breasts
For fresh nail marks
Adorned them with the lotuses of her eyes
Which were mirrored in their smooth expanse. [150]

233

One moment she tried wiping,
The next scrubbing,
And after that rubbing.
The young wife was completely at a loss
What to do with the nail mark
Her husband had left on her breast.   [433]

234

Because she put up with it all
The clumsy youth went on making love to her
So that her limbs now look like wilting acacia flowers.   [56]

235

Look, mother-in-law!
That lovely mass of lotuses
Used to be the most beautiful thing in our village,
But now winter has made them look
Like a sesame field just after harvest.   [8]

236

Aunt,
Not a lotus is damaged,
Not a goose has been scared away,
But someone has pushed a cloud on its back
In the village pond.   [110]

237

Mother,
What's it to me
If the Narmadā lets the elephant bull
Beat her again and again with his trunk
And scrape and squeeze both her banks?   [549]

238

O emerald,
A succession of incompetent jewelers
Has ground you so long on the stone
That you are no bigger than a sesame seed.
So what's this talk about being valuable? [629]

239

While making love, women go on enticing men
Up to the very end
When their eyes,
Long and oval like the petals of the waterlily,
Close. [5]

240

By her wide open eyes,
By the sweat streaming down her cheeks,
The woman said without saying a word
That her part of the business was fulfilled. [828]

241

The wife who had already reached her climax
But did not realize that that was the end of that
Remained in a state of excitement
Expecting something more. [155]

242

Once the festival starts its glamor is over,
Like the full moon in broad daylight,
Like sex which in the end loses its savor,
Or like gratitude without a steady stream of gifts. [68]

243

The lamp was so absorbed
In looking at the young couple
Playfully making love
In all sorts of different positions
That it did not notice that the oil had run out.   [548]

244

Wet and fragrant after her bath
And with flowers falling from it,
She lays her long, thick hair
On her exhausted husband's chest
After a summer afternoon
Of making love.   [299]

245

Decent wives, who feel abashed
When love is over
But cannot find their skirts,
Hastily cover their naked thighs
By embracing their husbands once again.   [459]

246

How could I not remember that man
Who even after it was over
Looked at my limp body
As if he felt like doing it again?   [413]

247

After making love,
He took a step, then turned
And took me in his arms again.

That moment I felt what it was to be a wife whose
 husband is abroad
And he what it was to be that woman's husband.   [98]

THE PERFECT WIFE

The perfect wife does not embarrass her husband or his family by loud quarrels or extravagant wishes. The latter can be a problem when she is pregnant and has to eat for two (252). Also, when her relatives visit her, bringing generous presents, she is expected to refuse them and thereby show that she is well taken care of by her husband (254). A really good wife also knows how to wake her husband early in the morning and put him in the right mood (256).

248

Those who know what is good for the household
And what isn't,
Know what it can put up with
And what it can't
—Those are proper wives.
The rest are a drain on men. [513]

249

Instead of criticism smiles,
Instead of grievances extreme politeness,
Instead of quarrels tears,
Such is the way of good wives. [514]

250

Laughing without showing her teeth,
Moving around without crossing the threshold,

Looking without raising her face:
Such is the way of a virtuous wife. [526]

251

The poorer, the uglier, the more decrepit
Her husband becomes
The more a true woman loves him. [293]

252

Every time her poor in-laws ask her
What she would most like to eat,
The pregnant wife,
Anxious not to cause embarrassment to her husband,
Simply says: "Water." [472]

253

When her friends asked the young wife
Who was pregnant for the first time
What she craved most
She simply looked at her husband. [15]

254

Protecting the self-image of her husband,
Who is poor but proud of his breeding,
The wife scorns her own relatives
As they arrive with rich presents. [38]

255

Conscious of the family's situation,
The pregnant wife does not mention what she craves for
But keeps it to herself,
Like an indecent proposal made by one of her husband's
    brothers. [290]

256

The sun is already shining
When the good wife
Takes hold of her husband's feet
And gives them a shake.
Since she is smiling
A smile appears on his grumpy face.   [130]

THE BROTHER-IN-LAW

After marriage the wife becomes part of the household of her husband's family, which usually includes a number of younger, unmarried brothers. These young men like hanging around the young wife, teasing her, and making all kinds of sexual innuendo. The wife cannot really complain about this to her husband as it could lead to the much-dreaded breakup of the household (257).

To one of these young men, who has become too importunate, the woman depicted in 260 recounts an episode from the *Rāmāyaṇa* epic, where Lakṣmaṇa, left behind with his elder brother's wife, Sītā, does not lay a finger on her. But the wife's good intentions can easily be misunderstood: the mere fact that she spends so much time in her brother-in-law's company may put all kinds of ideas into the young man's head.

257

She does not complain to her husband
About his brother's advances
Not because she herself has impure thoughts
But because he is so touchy
And she is afraid of causing a split in the family.
Instead she pines away.   [59]

258

How will you ever manage to kindle the fire
In the kitchen dark with smoke

With your young brother-in-law at your side
Trying to kiss the lotus of your mouth? [734]

259

Look at you:
Your eyes are red,
Tears flow down your cheeks,
And your heavy breasts are shaking.
You'd better stop
Trying to kindle the kitchen fire. [735]

260

The good wife takes all day
To explain to her importunate young brother-in-law
The paintings on the walls of their house
That depict the adventures of Lakṣmaṇa
Rāma's devoted younger brother. [35]

261

My dear man,
Why scan the sky
If it's crescent moons you're after?
Try looking at your sister-in-law's shoulder:
You'll find a whole row of them there. [571]

262

Tell me, brother-in-law,
That dog who fawned on the bitch
So persistently,
Where did he learn to turn his back on her
The moment he'd had his way? [690]

263

Mother-in-law,
The only trumpetflower tree in the village

Is at the headman's house,
Yet my brother-in-law's head
Is covered with trumpetflowers.
How strange!   [469]

264

Before her husband's eyes
The brazen woman passionately kissed his brother's mouth.
She said she did so because he'd said
That her mouth smelt of drink.   [872]

RIVAL WIVES

If he can afford it, the husband has more than one wife. However, every new acquisition means that his other wives have one more rival for their husband's attention. And they are only too aware that they cannot compete with a young girl whose breasts are still firm (266). Yet they do their best to remain attractive to their husband and to that end bathe in the freezing waters of the river on the day of the festival. The youngest wife does not join them but just looks on: she has no need to torture herself like that (274). On the other hand, she seems not to recognize how privileged she is to be the favorite wife. Otherwise, after the birth of her first child, she would not tell the other wives that she has had enough of being the favorite. They laugh, for they know better (273).

265

As the wedding day draws near
He can think only of making love
With his new bride.
The pleasures once shared
With his first wife
No longer find a place in his heart. [479]

266

When she saw the high breasts
Of her husband's new wife

The first wife sighed
And her face fell.   [382]

267

The more the wife flaunts her delicious, young body
The thinner become her waist, her husband,
And her rivals.   [292]

268

Among the other flowers in a garland
The scent of the young jasmine will never get lost:
There is something unusually powerful
About the damned thing.   [281]

269

After tasting to the full the pleasures of love
The young wife slept soundly,
Unaware how her weary limbs
Were a torture to her rivals.   [717]

270

The red
That during the night her husband
Removed from her lips
Appears the next morning
In her co-wives' sleepless eyes.   [106]

271

Normally one gives away things
Of which one has a surplus.
But to your husband's other wives you give
Something that is not yours to give:
Unhappiness.   [212]

272

Your heart is made of nectar,
Your hands allay the yearning of those who yearn,
Where, O moon-faced girl,
Do you produce the heat
With which you burn your enemies? [726]

273

The attractive wife,
Who had just given birth for the first time,
Made everyone laugh
When she kept on saying that she had had enough
Of being called her husband's favorite. [123]

274

When her rivals take a freezing cold bath
Before dressing for the festival,
The youngest wife shows her privileged position
By not bothering. [79]

275

See how the young cow makes plain her favored position:
In the middle of the pen
She rubs her eyelid
Against the horn of the vicious bull. [460]

276

The bull lives only for you
And the heifers only for the bull,
So please, dear cow, stay alive
For the life of our herd
Depends on your life. [640]

THE ERRANT HUSBAND

The wife has not only her husband's other wives to compete with. After a while his interest in her wanes and to her great grief she discovers she is not the only woman in his mind and heart (287). In fact his heart seems to be so crowded with women that the only way to slip into it again is to make herself as thin as possible (288). Having no really effective means of getting him back, she consoles herself with the thought that the more women he meets, the more he may begin to appreciate her (277).

The wife is now in the position where she has to be grateful for every visit her husband pays her, even if he does so purely out of politeness and good breeding. She welcomes illness or fever because it brings him to her to enquire about her health (294). The result, though, is that on top of his infidelities she has to put up with his polite conversation (298). At the same time she has to reassure him when in the morning he wakes up beside her and looks around distraught, unsure of his surroundings and the identity of the woman beside him (304).

277

O god, please
Let my husband form other attachments,
For men who have experience of one person only
No longer appreciate what's good and what's bad. [48]

278

While making love to another woman
His beloved will come to mind
Both when he sees and doesn't see
A familiar trait.   [44]

279

I agree, my dear,
She is a model of virtue and beauty,
And, yes,
I am quite worthless.
But, tell me,
Must everyone not up to her standard
Be condemned to death?   [512]

280

Maybe my talents are slight,
Maybe for him talents mean nothing,
Maybe I have no talents
And he knows someone who has.   [203]

281

My boy,
I've so often described how nice you are
To those sly hussies
That it's my fault you're now beyond my reach.
Whom else can I blame?   [350]

282

Mother,
They snatch my husband from me
As if he were a dish of plums in a blind man's hands.

At the same time they are jealous of me:
A hood is growing out of the snake's tail! [240]

283

How much happiness
Can my errant husband get
From the sidelong glances
Cast by women starved of love? [582]

284

You love her,
I love you,
She hates you,
And you hate me.
I speak plainly
Since love is full of complications. [126]

285

I have both you
And your new love
To bear in my heart.
How dare you ask, you fool,
Why I am wasting away?
Even an ox collapses when overloaded. [275]

286

You live in my heart
With your wife locked in your own
For tell me how else could she know exactly what
    I want? [337]

287

She dwells in your heart,
In your eyes and in your dreams,

Where then, Mr Handsome,
Is there room for a poor wretch like me? [947]

288

Finding no room
Among the thousands of women
That crowd your heart,
She does nothing else each day
But make her thin body even thinner. [182]

289

You abide in my heart
And never trouble it.
Yet, for all my affection,
I lose faith, as girls do,
And grow suspicious. [509]

290

These indifferent side glances of yours,
Which turn this way and that
But take no notice of me,
Cut me to the quick. [146]

291

As long as you are within sight
My beautiful man, you give pleasure.
But as soon as you are out of sight
You cause such grief
That I never want to see you again. [727]

292

Aunt,
He looks at me now with blank eyes,

Without a trace of jealousy or anger,
As if I were just anybody.
So how can I help growing thin?   [507]

293

When people ask me,
In your presence,
Why my body grows thinner by the day,
I don't know what to say to whom.   [347]

294

By bringing that man
Who keeps his distance
To ask me how I'm feeling,
You have proved a blessing.
Now, fever, if you take my life,
I will not complain.   [50]

295

Why should anyone care
Whether my fever has abated or not?
You, my dear, asking how I am
And smelling so fragrant,
Do not touch me who stink of fever.   [51]

296

Though you visit us only out of courtesy,
You rejoice our heart.
What delight you must give to those
Whom you visit with genuine fondness.   [85]

297

Doing your best out of politeness
To be nice to the likes of us,

In your heart you must be thinking
"To hell with politeness." [945]

298

Believe me, my dear,
The wrongs you have done me
Are nothing like as hurtful
As these polite words devoid of true feeling. [353]

299

Being separated from what is dear
And being forced to look at what isn't
Are two causes of grief.
I bow to your good breeding
Which demands that you act as you do. [24]

300

Go and leave me
To my tears and sighs,
Lest you suffer the same as I
When she leaves you
On account of your showing me
Such consideration. [944]

301

Aunt,
The words may be the same
But they sound quite different
Depending on whether they are said with affection
Or with reserve. [450]

302

O Sun,
What a precious sight,

What a feast for the eyes,
When you return at dawn
Red all over
Having spent the night elsewhere.
Ornament of the sky,
Lord of the day,
We bow before you humbly.   [655]

303

How the young beauty's face grows dark
When, with a furtive glance, she sees
The plowman flaunting an ear ornament
Of rose-apple leaves.   [180]

304

It's your own wife:
You can embrace her.
Suddenly awoken by cockcrow,
You look around distraught
As if you'd spent the night
In another man's house,
But don't be alarmed:
It's your own.   [583]

GETTING HER NAME WRONG

The husband with all his wives and mistresses cannot always tell them apart, so that not infrequently he addresses one of them by the wrong name. In order to save the situation, the wife is told to treat it as just a trick of her husband to see what she looks like when jealous (306), or else the mother-in-law warns her son that his wife may pay him back in his own coin (307). She may even take pity on the woman whose name has, as it were, been stolen (308). Or she may sarcastically accuse her husband of old-fashioned honesty (311). But after a series of humiliations such a slip of the tongue can prove to be the final blow (305).

305

Just look!
After her husband had addressed her with his mistress's name
The ornaments she had put on for the fair
Suddenly appeared like a garland on the head of a buffalo
Being led to sacrifice. [496]

306

Hey! you angry girl,
Don't you see
That when he calls you by the wrong name
It's only because he wants to see your eyes
Rolling with jealousy? [908]

307

My son, don't overdo
That joke of calling her by another woman's name.
Your wife also knows how to be funny.   [907]

308

Have you no feelings?
How can she enjoy your favor
At the same time as me
When you rob her of her name
And give it to me?   [452]

309

Is that to be my name?
Use it, darling, use it:
Don't be embarrassed.
If my name doesn't appeal to you
What use is it to me?   [905]

310

Foolish girl, you're in a muddle.
His getting your name wrong
Is nothing to cry about.
What do you think?
With those big eyes
He could never have made such a mistake.   [909]

311

What good old-fashioned honesty!
But really, my dear,
You're the only one who goes in for it.
Nowadays people think one thing and say another.   [32]

LOVERS' QUARRELS

In poem 374 a sulking couple is compared to a pair of wrestlers, each watching for the other to make the first move. One possible outcome is depicted in the next poem (375), when both simultaneously burst out laughing, whereas in 316 the situation remains unresolved: she is too offended to make any move and her husband is immobilized by guilt. In 351 the woman has definitely gone too far: she drives her hitherto innocent husband into doing the very things she accuses him of. After a good quarrel love tastes new, but unless one stops at the right moment it can end in total estrangement (355). The trick is to determine exactly when that moment is: if one relents too soon, one makes oneself ridiculous and foregoes the pleasure of a passionate reunion (341); if too late, one will suffer for the rest of one's life (398).

To show that she is offended the wife has a whole range of possibilities at her disposal. For instance, she can insist on strict propriety even when she is alone with her husband (318), avoid looking at him (335), or talk about everyday matters after they have had a terrible row (317). Some of the things the wife does have an effect contrary to that intended: frowning and crying only make her face the more attractive (322, 323).

It is not always easy to sustain the role of angry wife. To think about sulking is one thing, to do so in her husband's presence another (331). Sometimes the quarrel is resolved unconsciously, as when the wife, who has angrily turned her back on her husband in bed, turns over again in sleep (370).

The man has to play along. The worst thing he can do is insist on his authority (344). He simply has to do a little groveling. But sometimes he cannot conceal the fact that he is enjoying it: the tears of resentment shed by his wife standing over him raise gooseflesh on his back (347). He knows that his groveling is the last stage in the game and that his wife will soon come round. Lovers' quarrels are indeed a form of psychological warfare, but sulking after all is a sign of love (313), and living together is anyhow not for the over-sensitive (356).

312

First let my dear husband come home,
Then let me give him a scolding,
And then let him do his best to bring me round.
There must be someone who can get all three wishes. [17]

313

Where there is no wakefulness,
Jealousy, strife, sulking,
And good old flattery,
There no love is either. [829]

314

Sudden outbursts of anger and the next moment calm,
Constant pretence as well as agonies of jealousy,
Such, my son, is the nature of love. [677]

315

If I think again of those days
When I acted as though I were hurt
And you tried to pacify me
As if I were really angry,
I have to cry
And am unable to become angry. [941]

316

Those weighed down by the burden of sulking
Cannot move
And obviously he feels too guilty to come.
So I am waiting for someone
Who, unasked and of his own accord,
Will bring him to me or me to him. [932]

317

A sulking woman
Does not hurt so much by silence
As by small talk
After overwhelming anger. [565]

318

She knows how to give expression
To what remains of the anger he tried to conciliate
By acting with reserve
Even when they are alone together. [88]

319

The grief and anger they suffer
At the moment they hear about their husbands' lapses
Do not make young women cry so loud
As when the husbands appear in person
And ask to be forgiven. [915]

320

That jealous anger which my friends,
Having found a slit,
Managed to lodge in my heart,
Sneaked away like a lover
At the sight of my husband. [144]

321

That you did not look at him
When he looked at you,
That you did not speak to him
While you are usually so forthright,
That you did not want to show him kindness
—Our clever friends have noted it all. [720]

322

Young girl,
Wipe away these tears
Which make your face look even more attractive,
For he might do it again,
Thinking how well they suit you. [683]

323

Long-eyed girl,
The effect of your anger
Was completely annulled
By the unusual beauty of your face
As you frowned. [920]

324

Intently the husband gazed at the stream of tears
First reflecting the color of his angry wife's eyes,
Then of her cheeks, and then of her lips.
It looked like a rainbow,
Except that it was straight. [808]

325

The lover wipes away the silver moonbeams
Blending with the blue gleams of her sapphire earrings

From the face of his offended mistress,
Mistaking them for tears mixed with eye-black. [302]

326

See how the affronted wife
Is washing away the dark patches of the moon
Reflected on her cheek
With an endless stream of water
From the jars of her eyes. [280]

327

Be off!
Stop wiping away my tears!
Crying is what my stupid eyes were made for.
For when they tried looking they got distracted
And failed to see your true nature. [706]

328

Words which come from the heart
Sound different.
Get away with you!
I've no time for words
That pay mere lip service. [451]

329

You allow me to see you
And still speak kindly.
But, my dear, is this
The way to behave?
For who would break a heart
And having broken it
Still show his face? [489]

330

Don't think winter is content
Merely to wither the summer jasmine.
It also has to produce a mass
Of worthless winter jasmine.   [426]

331

When he's not here
My mind is full of his thousand offenses,
But the moment I see him,
Dear friend,
I can't think of a single one.   [903]

332

How dare you!
And which offenses am I supposed to forgive,
My darling:
Those you have committed,
Those you are committing,
Or those you are about to commit?   [90]

333

Only after you had won her round
Did she start to make a count of your offenses.
When the fingers of both hands proved not enough
The poor thing finally burst into tears.   [277]

334

A man who is angry at one's being bossy
Can be won round in due course,
But someone who is angry at one's being servile
How can I appease him?   [488]

335

I'll frown at him,
I'll abuse him,
And I'll turn my back on him.
I'll do whatever you say, friends,
As long as I don't have to look at him.   [743]

336

How wayward of you:
The more a woman detests you
The more you like her.
Though I know this all too well
There is nothing I can do
About this cursed love of mine.   [511]

337

When he misbehaves
I cannot get angry with him,
Not even in jest,
Not with this body
That seems to be on loan
And not mine to command.   [195]

338

My heart,
If you have to burn, burn,
If you have to boil, boil,
And if you have to break, break.
As for me,
I am completely through with that traitor.   [401]

339

The only reason I do not die of anger
This very moment, my dear,

Is that in my next life
I do not wish to be dependent on you again
Because I died thinking of you. [375]

340

If you cannot live without the man,
You'd better stay on good terms with him
Whatever wrong he may have done.
Even after the town has gone up in flames
One cannot do without fire. [163]

341

Stupid woman,
Because you stopped being angry
The moment he stood before you
You missed a lot of fun:
He would have had to fall at your feet
And cover you with hot, impetuous kisses. [465]

342

I will never forget,
Once when he lay in silence at my feet,
What pleasure I got from twisting his hair round my toe
And pulling hard. [108]

343

By disentangling her husband's hair
From the clasp of her anklet
As he lies at her feet,
She tells him
That pride has left her heart. [188]

344

Women only like men
Who mask their authority

And grovel like slaves
At their angry lovers' feet.
All the rest make pitiful husbands. [91]

345

Ah, the horrors I have to witness
By staying alive:
Him groveling in front of me
And my wretched self giving in to it. [930]

346

Be reasonable!
Your husband has fallen at your feet.
Why not help him up again?
However long your love has lasted,
This could be the end. [390]

347

Believe me,
I would not believe you
If these tears that I weep
Were not pierced by the gooseflesh
Rising on your back
As you kneel before me. [216]

348

As her lover begs
To be kicked on the head,
The angry woman
Stops her foot in midair
And sheds big tears. [916]

349

Have you no shame?
Get away, go and fawn on the woman

Who, with the lac on her toenail,
Put this red dot
On your forehead. [946]

350

From her face to your face
And from your face to my feet,
Going from one to the other,
The dot painted on her forehead
Has performed a real miracle. [179]

351

How stupid!
She was so anxious to taste the pleasure of being groveled to
That she made out that he had done something
When he hadn't,
And led her innocent lover into devious ways. [306]

352

Why storm off
Trailing your skirt behind you?
Slow down!
Aren't you afraid your waist might break
Under the weight of your breasts? [160]

353

When he ran out of the house,
Dismayed at my rudely rejecting
His attempt at reconciliation,
You should have stopped him
Instead of laughing at someone else's misfortune. [420]

354

Face to face and right in front of your rival
He begged you: "Be nice to me again."

What more do you expect
From persisting in your anger? [927]

355

After every quarrel, it's true,
The pleasures of love taste new.
But, proud woman,
Too much of this pride
And his love will be destroyed. [522]

356

Say what you like:
I can take it.
For being touchy
And living with the man one loves
Are two things that don't go together. [904]

357

Love based on pretence,
Love based on force,
Love based on greed,
Love based on compliance
—Honor to them all! [744]

358

Aunt,
When the tree of love,
Rooted in long affection,
Is struck by the axe of pride
It falls without a sound. [431]

359

When he knelt at your feet
You took no notice,

When he spoke affectionately
You answered curtly,
When he went away
You did not try to stop him.
Tell me,
What exactly do you hope to gain
By your pride?   [432]

360

You there, with the big breasts
Propping your face up,
Pay attention to what I say:
Youth does not last forever.
So don't look down your nose
At your lover.   [924]

361

Silly girl,
Youth races past
Like a river in spate,
The days are fleeting
And the nights unreturning.
So why this stubborn sulkiness?   [45]

362

Life is transient,
Youth passes never to return,
Tomorrow is not the same as today.
So why are people so stubborn?   [247]

363

Give as much affection
As you can muster.

For not everyone can bear to suffer
The withdrawal of kindness.   [71]

364

Slender girl,
The parts of your body that used to be plump
Have become thin,
And those that were thin
Are now tiny.
What is the use of keeping so aloof?   [309]

365

Don't make your rivals happy:
When your lover is eager to please you,
Humor him,
For, dear girl,
By doling out oversize portions of disdain
You will dwindle to nothing.   [152]

366

To make sure she didn't look like a widow
Her friends constantly hitched up
The sulking girl's fallen bangle
As though they were bangle sellers.   [540]

367

Proud lady, silently weeping,
Do not scold your arms
For straying into the empty hollow
That was your lover's embrace.   [354]

368

Imagining how it was when her lover was with her,
The woman suddenly remembered how angry she had been

And raged against thin air.
Far from laughing, her friends wept for her. [60]

369

What do you think you are doing,
Embracing me from behind?
First you set fire to my heart
And then you start burning my back
With these hot sighs of remorse. [33]

370

Wrapped in her feelings of resentment
She turned her lovely face away
And fell fast asleep on our bed.
But continuing the tiff in dream
She turned away again
And so came face to face with me. [911]

371

I will never forget
How at first she turned her back on me,
Then, as her sulkiness faded,
Heaved up her round breasts,
While feigning sleep
—What pleasure it was to fondle them. [368]

372

You would not be so touchy
If you knew the pain of falling asleep beside one's lover
And waking up in the middle of the night
To discover that the bed is empty. [26]

373

If when he's away
One lies awake,

Grows pale,
And sighs deeply,
What is the point of being angry
When he's back again? [374]

374

After the quarrel neither give in
But feigning sleep, lie still,
Hold their breath and listen.
Who will win the bout? [27]

375

When their surreptitious glances met
The couple whom I thought were sulking
Both burst out laughing. [702]

376

This is just a show of anger:
There is no cause for it at all.
Besides, you're covered with gooseflesh.
Anyone can see, silly girl,
That what you want is the pleasure
Of a passionate embrace. [929]

377

Proud lady,
When he approached you
You relentlessly turned away,
But the gooseflesh on your back
Shows that in your heart
You are prepared to face him again. [87]

378

At the mention of his name you bristle;
At the sound of his voice your anger melts;

Seeing him face to face, you tremble.
What will you do when you embrace?   [661]

379

You fool,
What makes you think I'm angry?
Stop your needless groveling
And take me in your arms.
What's the point in my sulking?
It only makes you angry.   [184]

380

No, you are not to blame, my dear,
It's the fault of my own fond eyes
That let you into my heart,
And of my heart
That does not know how to sulk.   [942]

381

Do your worst, have no fear:
I can take anything from you, my dear.
In my heart, so brimful of your virtues,
There is no room for any faults.   [376]

382

You fool,
My own life means more to me than you do.
Therefore, if I give in to your anger
It is only because without you I have no life.   [215]

383

I will do my best to avoid
Doing the things you don't like,

But, my dear,
What can I do about the things
I don't like?   [617]

384

How are you to blame?
It is my wretched heart that is hard.
You always look me straight in the eye,
Always speak gently,
And never turn your back on me.   [943]

385

Calm down.
    Who's the angry one?
You, my slim beauty.
    How can one be angry with a stranger?
Who's the stranger?
    You, my lord.
How come?
    I must have done something wrong in a past life.   [384]

386

Who would not love to be tough on a cringing husband
But for the long winter nights
That erode one's pride?   [745]

387

I will never forget
How, for all her resentment,
She dropped off to sleep
At my feet,
After a day of household chores
Performed in angry silence.   [226]

388

How is this pride going to stand its ground
At the sight of the beloved's face
If it is already alarmed
By the burgeoning buds of the *aṃkolla*? [778]

389

That my sulking mood,
Which was completely justified,
Disappeared just like that,
Is entirely your doing,
Aṃkolla plant,
As you unexpectedly started to blossom. [779]

390

This mango bud
Hanging from her ear,
Like a dear friend whispering good advice,
Succeeds in banishing sulkiness,
However justified it may be. [783]

391

See how the woman's indignation at her husband
Escapes with a soft sigh
Like sand from a clenched fist. [74]

392

When he kisses her passionately on the mouth
The red flush of anger disappears from her face
Like wine draining from a crystal goblet. [933]

393

Turning her face upwards
With his cupped hands,

Her husband offers her wine
—One mouthful to drink
As a medicine
For sulkiness. [270]

394

While he was blowing on the hand
That still stung from the slap I gave him,
I could not help laughing
And put my other hand around his neck. [86]

395

Tears were still running down her cheeks and lips
When, with a shy laugh, she said:
"But why am I still angry
When our love has reached the stage of swearing
    fidelity?" [519]

396

When their little son
Climbed on her husband's back
As he knelt at her feet,
She could not help laughing
Despite her fierce anger. [11]

397

Love
Estranged and patched up again,
Once its dissolution is plain to see,
Will never taste right again
Like water that has boiled then cooled. [53]

398

Proud woman,
Here on earth two ways are open

To people who are proud and haughty:
Either they find a treasure
Or they are pilgrims of love
For the rest of their lives.   [752]

THE FAITHLESS WIFE

The wife has far fewer opportunities to have an affair than her husband. For a start, it is very difficult for her to leave the house and escape the watchful eye of her mother-in-law (407). This can lead to smuggling her lover into the house and risking discovery by her husband should he return home unexpectedly (401). She is also more or less limited to men who happen to visit the house, such as the barber (405). The barber, though, deals with body waste and is very low caste, which makes an affair with him a grievous offense (404). Should the wife escape from the house, she cannot go very far. One possible meeting place is beneath the village banyan tree. But its privacy is destroyed when wayfarers threaten to cut the hanging roots to let in more light, or when the tree itself loses its leaves (413, 414). Spring, with its associations of love, is particularly hard to endure for a wife permanently imprisoned within the house and starved of sympathy (407, 409). She feels like the ship's crow, which, failing to spy land, has no option but to return to the ship (422).

399

The reason why your wife is faithful
And we are unfaithful to our husbands,
Is obvious, my dear:
There isn't another young man like you. [228]

400

With food and water
The false woman has trained the dog

To welcome her lover
And bark at her husband as he comes home.   [664]

401

"My lord,
This man seeks shelter with us.
Do look after him."
With these words the wife hastily introduced her lover
To her husband
Who had returned home unexpectedly.   [297]

402

Before her husband's very eyes
Her sharp friends pick up the young wife
And carry her, arms adangle,
To her healer-lover's house,
Saying: "She's been bitten by a scorpion."   [237]

403

As soon as her husband took her on his lap
Sweat poured from her
Like an attentive servant,
Washing the mud of last night's assignation
From her feet.   [767]

404

You're right, I am a loose woman
And you are virtuous.
So you stay clear
Before you tarnish your reputation.
But I at least don't lust after a barber
Like the wife of someone we know.   [417]

405

With one hand clutching at her skirt,
Which is slipping down,
And with the other her hair,
Which has come loose,
The housewife chases after her little son,
Who is running away, scared of the barber. [291]

406

The soup is burnt,
The chickpeas aren't roasted,
The young man has gone past,
And I am stuck in this house
With an angry mother-in-law.
It's like playing the flute to phantoms. [558]

407

The south wind blows strong,
Mother-in-law keeps me locked up indoors,
But someone who dies sniffing the scent of *aṃkolla*
Dies all the same. [497]

408

What makes you think I'm lying, you fool?
I know spring can do anything,
But the fragrant flowers of the amaranth
Have not made me in the least unfaithful. [219]

409

Mother-in-law!
There are no buds on the mango
And the south wind does not blow,

Yet the yearning in my heart
Tells me that spring is on its way. [543]

410

Slender girl,
Don't be so naïve:
Brush off your back
All trace of the leaves
From the *aṃkolla* in the yard,
Otherwise your clever sisters-in-law will start
    thinking. [313]

411

When she said:
"Daughter-in-law,
There are long bamboo leaves in your hair."
I said:
"Mother-in-law,
Your back is all white." [676]

412

The nasty dog is dead,
Mother-in-law is drunk,
My husband is out,
And the buffalo has broken the bolt.
Who is going to tell on us? [550]

413

Afraid that travelers
Might cut the hanging roots of the shady banyan
To let light in,
The faithless women stealthily spattered the leaves
With white. [166]

414

Aunt,
A yellow leaf, battered by the wind,
Falls from the village banyan
And with it the pale faces
Of the false women.   [295]

415

The plowman's wife bemoans the sesame field,
Bleached by the rays of the sun
And pockmarked by the burrowing of field mice.   [769]

416

River-nymph Narmadā,
Today I will put discretion aside
And tell your husband, the sea,
How you had a rendezvous with the stream
In a bower of reeds.   [760]

417

He is so jealous
That he does not want his wife
To gather sweetwood flowers at night.
Instead, the honest soul
Goes and gathers them himself.   [159]

418

Just gather the fallen flowers,   *(aloud)*
But do not shake the jasmine bush.
Your father-in-law can hear   *(whispered)*
The monotonous jingle of your bracelets.   [959]

419

A village full of young men,
Spring, youth, an aged husband,
Strong wine, nobody to tell you what to do:
The only way to avoid going astray
Is to die.   [197]

420

The winter nights are long,
For months your husband's been away,
So you must be sleeping well.
How odd that you should fall asleep by day.   [66]

421

The false woman bewailed her dead husband
With such choking sobs
That even her lover was afraid
She might join him on the pyre.   [873]

422

O! What a fool
Love has made of me,
As when the ship's crow
Circles the whole heaven
Only to settle on the ship again.   [746]

THE ABDUCTED WIFE

The abduction of women seems to have been not uncommon, but the relationship between the abducted woman and her kidnapper varies. She may fall in love with her young kidnapper (425), but he dares not take it any further for fear of her husband's revenge (423). Or else, overestimating her husband's capabilities and expecting to be liberated soon, she may refuse to escape even when an opportunity presents itself. Naturally the kidnapper has his own interpretation of her motives (426). Sometimes the captive woman is the dupe of her desires: mistaking a thunderclap for the twang of her husband's bow, she is confident of being rescued and reunited with him at any moment. The royal captives, who belong to the warrior class, know better (427, 428).

423

With fear and with longing
The kidnappers repeatedly steal glances
At the round breasts of the warrior's wife
As if they were pots of gold
Guarded by snakes. [577]

424

Bees pursue the mango blossom
That the scruffy farmhand has torn off with his nails

And placed on his head,
Like young men thronging around a woman
Taken hostage. [331]

425

Though distressed by the death of her relatives
The hostage made eyes at her kidnapper
Who was a handsome youth.
For who begrudges anyone
His good points? [118]

426

Why aren't you trying to escape?
What makes you so confident,
That you remain calm?
With a smile the bowman's wife replies:
"You will soon find out, kidnapper!" [528]

427

It is only the echo of a thunderclap
From an early rain cloud.
I suppose you were hoping it might be the twang
Of your husband's bow,
For why else is the hair on your body bristling? [55]

428

Thinking she hears the twang of her husband's bow
Above the crashing thunder,
The captive wife tells the royal hostages
To wipe away their tears. [54]

DEPARTURE

A large number of poems deal with the theme of separation due to the husband's travels abroad. Whatever the reason for these travels may be—they are not specified—it is clear that the husband cannot afford not to go away. Unless one shows initiative, poverty, starvation and death will follow (430). The hardships of the wayfarer and the grief of the deserted wife are a constant theme. The wayfarer suffers from cold in winter, heat in summer, and wet in the rainy season that makes the roads impassable. His wife grows so thin that her bracelets slip off her arms and she grows pale. Life becomes so unbearable for her that death would be a relief. The poems in this section focus on the moment of departure itself. We see, for instance, how the husband searches for any excuse to postpone his departure. He cannot set off on a Tuesday, which is an inauspicious day, or when it rains (429). The sight of his wife's pale face and her arms, which have grown thin, make him even more irresolute. At the same time his wife tries desperately to prevent him from leaving. She does not let go when she embraces him (432), and he has to wrench himself from her grip (438). Another trick is to place a fresh mango shoot on the customary bowl of water offered to her husband on departure (431). The mango shoot should remind him of spring, the month that in India is particularly associated with love and lovemaking.

429

The would-be traveler has become so addicted to the
pleasant pastime

Of fondling his wife's firm breasts
That he welcomes any bad omen
—Wishes it were Tuesday or a day of rain. [261]

430

If a man shows initiative
There is the prospect of either wealth or death.
Even if he lacks initiative, death is certain,
Wealth is not. [42]

431

Foolish girl, do not cry.
A fresh mango shoot with its new blossom
Placed on the mouth of the farewell bowl
Will surely stop your lover departing. [143]

432

As the wife embraced her husband
Who was about to depart,
The bracelets slipped from her slender arms
Clasped around his neck
And fell at his feet like shackles. [786]

433

Seeing his wife's face grow pale
As he bade her farewell
The husband could not bring himself to leave,
His feet fettered by affection. [501]

434

As her husband is about to depart
She goes from door to door

Asking all the women who suffer from absent husbands
For the secret of surviving the farewell. [47]

435

Dear friend,
Allow me this one day of crying.
Tomorrow, I promise,
When he has left
And if I'm still alive,
I will cry no more. [503]

436

That their husbands blithely go abroad
Is the fault of their wives.
The moment one or two of them die
There will be no more talk of separation. [587]

437

How frustrated he must feel
To threaten to leave again.
It makes his young wife languish
As though she'd been given a drug. [111]

438

Having wrenched yourself from my grip
You left for the road,
But only when you manage to escape from my heart as well
Will I acknowledge your power. [749]

THE TRAVELER'S WIFE

The husband usually departs immediately after the rainy season, promising to be back before the rains start again. For once the rains begin, travel is virtually impossible and there is little chance of his wife seeing him again soon. The wife usually keeps count of the days of her husband's absence either with her fingers and toes (447) or by drawing lines on a wall of her house (443, 501). Without her husband the days and nights seem as long as eons. The only pastimes available to her are looking out for her husband and dreaming of him, but these are spoiled by her tears and her sleeplessness (451). She also grows so thin that her bracelets become too wide and threaten to slip off her arms. Without them she looks like a widow. Seeing the wife without bracelets is especially shocking to her mother-in-law who, generally quite insensitive to the sufferings of her daughter-in-law, infers from this that her son has died abroad (461, 489). The wife grows so thin that the people around her fear she might actually die. Her friends keep a close watch on her by night, listening out for every sign of life, and try to comfort and divert her by day (458, 459, 464).

Each season of the year adds its special torment to the wife's already desperate condition. Spring reminds her of love and lovemaking (478, 480), and the summer heat makes her even thinner than she already is (482). At the first sight of rain clouds in the west the wife starts decorating herself in anticipation of her husband's homecoming (494). Yet the very same rain clouds increase her desperation, and once the rains have truly begun and the traveler husband has still not returned, the situation becomes really hopeless.

In several poems the woman is depicted sitting alone or with her baby son in a house with a leaking roof (for example, 493).

In some poems we see how the wife tries to write a letter to her absent husband but does not know what to write or else is incapable of doing so. Throughout his absence she goes to the door or to the porch to look out for him. In two poems her full round breasts are compared to the two pots filled with water which are traditionally placed at the door to welcome a guest (496, 497). Her face above her breasts is compared to a lotus placed on these water pots and her long eyes to lotus petals scattered on the street. In another poem (502) the woman begs her left eye to tremble, which is considered a good omen. She promises that as soon as her husband arrives she will close her right eye, granting her left one the exclusive pleasure of looking at him.

During her husband's absence the wife is expected to behave with modesty. As a token she has to keep her long hair tied in a bun. The hair may be untied or hang loose again only after his return (442, 508). Some women, however, go wild the moment their husband has departed. They seem to have been waiting for it: the very same day they make themselves attractive and stay up late (441) or try to attract the attention of the man next door (444). But such a woman may be in for a surprise. For what is she to make of the fact that, after her husband's departure, the woman next door also starts crying, counting the days and growing thin (446)?

439

They fell on my ear
And struck at my heart
—Oh what more can I suffer?—
Your parting words: "I'm off."   [831]

440

Today he is gone,
Today the alleys are empty,

The temples are empty,
The crossroads are empty,
And so is my heart. [190]

441

Only today he departed,
And today his women stay up late
Dyeing the banks of the Godā
Yellow with turmeric soap. [58]

442

When the lovely woman had finished her bath
Her hair,
Which had known the pleasure
Of touching her buttocks,
Started to weep drops of water
At the thought of being tied into a bun again. [556]

443

"Today he has left."
"Today he has left."
"Today he has left."
Already on the very first morning
She covered the whole wall with lines. [208]

444

It is pitch-dark outside,
My husband left today,
And the house is deserted.
Please, neighbor, do keep watch:
I don't want to be burgled. [335]

445

Young and attractive and her husband abroad,
Living in poverty at a busy crossroad,

With loose women in the neighborhood,
—You're not telling me she's still chaste? [36]

446

She shares my tears,
Counts off each day,
And grows as thin as I do
While my husband is away.
Aunt, the concern my neighbor shows
Is quite extraordinary. [848]

447

Having passed the time
By counting the days
First on her fingers, then on her toes,
The young girl burst into tears,
Not knowing what to count with next. [307]

448

The tear mixed with eye-black
Looks like a line drawn around her heart
To guide the saw of separation
In its agonizing surgery. [153]

449

Anxious about the stream of tears
Rolling down her face
At the thought of her absent husband,
She turns her head aside
As she puts down the lamp. [222]

450

Drenched by tears,
Scorched by long, hot sighs,

Her lips in your absence
Perform the penance of fire and water. [185]

451

As she can't sleep when you are away
She is deprived of the pleasure of seeing you in her dreams,
And her tears spoil the pastime of looking out for you. [487]

452

How much longer can I go on
In this misery,
My will to live dependent
On visualizing your face
In my imagination? [339]

453

In whatever direction I gaze I see your image before me.
The whole horizon is like a panorama with paintings of you
    alone. [531]

454

Happy the women
Who at least see their lovers in dream.
But without him I cannot sleep
Let alone dream. [397]

455

Let her sit with eyes closed,
Dreaming of her husband.
For until he returns
What is there for her to look at
With her eyes open? [842]

456

The pleasures of love,
Which gave the women such complete delight,
Are chewed over and endlessly regurgitated
Once their husbands have gone abroad. [670]

457

Stirring the Ocean of Milk, which is my heart,
With the churning stick of separation
You have rooted out the pearls of my joys. [475]

458

To help the young wife bear being parted
Her ingenious friends tell her tales
Of lovers' long absences,
Listing the various ways they cause hurt,
Some quite imaginary. [840]

459

In your absence, cruel man,
She is as helpless as a bird in the hands of a fowler
And is only kept alive by her understanding friends. [810]

460

Friend, tell me honestly, I beg of you,
Is it the case with all women
That the bracelets grow larger on their wrists
When their husband is away? [453]

461

Even her harsh mother-in-law
Was moved to tears when both the girl's bracelets

Slipped off as she fell at her feet,
So long had her husband been abroad.   [493]

462

Eyes shut,
She imagines her husband on the bed
And embraces herself
While the bracelets fall loose
Upon her thin arms.   [133]

463

The crow refuses the rice ball offered by the woman
Whose husband is abroad.
Seeing it stuck between the bracelet,
Which has slipped from her arm,
And the downturned palm of her hand,
The bird is wary of a trap.   [205]

464

The sound of her bracelets,
As the traveler's wife turns on her side
And weakly moves her hands,
Is enough to reassure her friends.   [283]

465

In this world,
Mother,
Love without deceit does not exist,
For who would separate
Or who, being separated,
Would survive?   [124]

466

Friends,
Why do you say:

"Don't die, only keep alive
And you'll see him once again"?
That may be practical advice
But it's not the way of love.   [619]

467

She knew no way
To stop the insistent, ever-increasing
Pain of being parted from her lover
Except by diverting herself
With death.   [349]

468

When my lover left for distant lands
My eyes found their way back home,
But my heart is still beside him
Going wherever he goes.   [660]

469

Sweet moon,
Crest jewel of the sky,
Beauty spot on the face of night,
Touch me with the very same rays
With which you've touched my most dearly beloved.   [16]

470

Each time she tries to write a letter
To her husband on his travels
The drops of sweat running down her pen
Blot out the syllables of his dear name.   [841]

471

Because my pen keeps slipping
In my clammy fingers

I can't even finish the word "Dear."
Friend, tell me,
How can I write the rest of my letter?   [244]

472

How can I put it in words?
One can say so little in a letter.
But the ache I feel in your absence
Is something you know of yourself.   [572]

473

Like being ill without a doctor,
Like being poor amongst one's relatives,
Like seeing one's enemy prosper,
This separation from you is intolerable.   [363]

474

For half the year the nights are long,
For the other half the days.
Separation confuses everything
As both its days and nights are long.   [846]

475

If you want to live long
Do not trouble about dubious elixirs.
Just arrange for your lover to go away,
Then the days grow long as eons.   [847]

476

"Go to sleep! It's past three o'clock!"
Dear girls, how can you say that to me?
The scent of jasmine makes sleep impossible.
Try going to sleep yourselves.   [412]

477

In spring
The clusters of jasmine
Bar the gate of the courtyard.
Even the comfort of looking down the road
Is denied to the grass widows. [322]

478

The mango puts out new shoots,
The fragrance of liquor fills the air,
An agreeable breeze is blowing from the south,
But business must mean more to him
And clearly he loves me no longer. [97]

479

Well? What do you mean, "Are you well?"
That stunted mango by the front door—
They tell me something nasty is coming out of
    its top. [499]

480

As though seizing the first sign of spring,
The south wind whirls the first *aṃkolla* leaf
Through the village streets. [777]

481

While her husband was abroad
The fierce midday sun
Did not torment the lonely wife
So much as the evening breeze
Wafting the scent of fresh acacia blooms. [839]

482

Since it is due to you
That she has grown thin
How could you jokingly ask her why?
"I usually do in summer" was her reply
Before she broke down.   [613]

483

People say that summer nights are short.
But I can't understand why they last so long
In the absence of my beloved.   [845]

484

Left on her own,
The poor woman has grown very thin,
The summer is almost over,
And her hardhearted husband is still abroad:
I don't know how this will end.   [806]

485

What you see are the heights of the Vindhya
Painted black by the forest fires of summer,
Not fresh rain clouds.
So do not worry about your husband's return.   [70]

486

Today,
As I think of the pleasures I've had
Without him,
The thunder of the first rain clouds
Sounds like the executioner's drum.   [29]

487

That she did not hear the thunder
Because she was swooning from the scent
Of the *kadamba* flower
Saved her life.
Otherwise the thunder would not have passed by
Without taking it.   [711]

488

Catch her!
No need to be afraid of this woman
Running around in circles:
She is not possessed by a demon,
Just a traveler's wife
Startled by a sudden thunderclap.   [386]

489

Without leaving her bedside for a moment
The mother nurses her daughter-in-law
Who has almost expired at the sight of the first rain clouds,
As if she were a medicine which could restore
The life of her son.   [336]

490

The storm snatched the thatch from the roof
And the lightning flashed through the rafters
As if to show the clouds the helpless wife,
Sitting in tears
Alone without her husband.   [315]

491

After the storm had ripped the straw from the roof
And rainwater streamed through the rafters,

The good lady tried to cover the wall with her hands
To protect the tally she'd made of her husband's
    absence. [170]

492

While rain trickled down
Through gaps in the thatch
The traveler's wife wept
And with her ceaseless flow of tears
Soaked the last dry spot in the house. [541]

493

With her head catching the water
That drips from the eaves
She protects her little son,
But does not notice that he is wet
With the tears she sheds
For her absent husband. [623]

494

Seeing clouds piling up in the west
The traveler's wife,
Who had despaired of her life,
Began to decorate her body
While tears streamed down her face. [539]

495

Foolish girl!
The clouds thunder,
The paths are grass-grown,
The rivers are swollen,
And still you look down the road
For your husband. [729]

496

Whom are you looking out for,
Standing at the door?
Your face above your prominent breasts
Looks like a lotus
Placed on top of the two water pots
Standing ready to welcome a guest. [256]

497

Leaning on the door
Looking out for you
She decorates the house for your return:
Her breasts two vases of plenty
And her eyes lotus petals strewn on the street. [140]

498

You fool,
It is on your account
That the poor girl sits patiently
Beneath the doorway
And, like the garland of welcome
Festooning it, wilts every day. [262]

499

Though its fragrance is gone,
She is still wearing the garland of jasmine you gave her,
Like a household god
In a deserted town. [194]

500

Heart,
At the time

When my lover mentioned the date of his return
You did not object.
So what are you doing now
Destroying our belief in his early arrival? [437]

501

Her friends,
Unsure when the final day would come,
Stealthily wiped out one or two strokes
Of her tally. [206]

502

O my left eye,
If my husband comes home today
Thanks to your quivering,
I will reward you with a good long look at him
While keeping my right eye tightly shut. [137]

503

More than his absence abroad
Or my wretchedness here at home
What pains me is my husband returning
Without quite reaching his goal. [76]

504

Her husband is at hand
And the festival in full swing.
Yet she delays putting on her jewels
To hearten the woman next door
Who is poor
And whose husband has still not returned. [39]

505

People running astray,
Hullabaloo everywhere,

Loud beating of drums:
The normal bustle of a festival
But oh! without him
More like a village fire.   [536]

506

"My daughter, stop crying.
He will come.
For he has never before missed today's fair."
With these empty words
She reassured her son's wife,
Turning her face away
To hide her tears.   [784]

507

As the woman from next door
Threw her arms around him
To welcome him home,
The wife's face grew dark
Despite her husband's return.   [849]

508

Ah, what a cruel man you are,
Thinking of leaving again
While the hair of my braid has not yet had time
To uncurl.   [273]

THE TRAVELER

When one sees the traveler dragging his feet on the very first day after his departure, one may wonder why he has left at all (509). All he does is gaze and groan and moan (510). But travel offers some compensation in the form of chance meetings with women along the way. We see the traveler accosting a young girl employed in the fields (512), and he has a brief romantic encounter in the house where he spends the night (513) or at the well where he has stopped to ask for water (516).

For the wayfarer, as for his wife at home, each season brings its own problems. In winter it is the cold, in spring it is the season's association with domestic happiness, in summer it is the heat. In the rainy season the *kadamba* blossom reminds him of his wife's pale cheek, and soon the roads will be completely impassable. If he wants to get home, he has to set off the moment he sees the first rain clouds. On his way back he imagines that the *kuṭaja* flowers, white like the teeth of someone laughing, are mocking him for being in such a hurry to return home that he fails to conclude his business (530).

509

On the very first day of his journey
The traveler stumbled,
Though the path was smooth,
As if hampered by the heavy buttocks
Of the wife he already missed.   [832]

510

Traveler,
Why did you ever leave home
If all you do is scan the horizon,
Sigh, yawn, moan, groan,
Faint, trip and stumble? [547]

511

The traveler had written nothing about himself
Nor asked how things were at home.
The palm leaf was covered all over with the syllables of his
    wife's name
Endlessly repeated. [833]

512

I won't go to the field.
What do I care if the parrots eat all the paddy.
Whenever I'm there
Travelers keep asking me the way
Which they know perfectly well. [821]

513

Here's my mother-in-law's bed,
Here is mine,
And there those of the servants.
Traveler, you won't see in the dark,
So do be careful not to fall into mine. [669]

514

The straw she had grudgingly given the traveler
To sleep on,
That same straw she was sweeping up next morning
In tears. [379]

515

Traveler,
If you ever want to see your wife again,
You'd better take another road.
For here in this wretched village
The landowner's daughter
In her desperation,
Is fishing with a very wide net.   [957]

516

For some time the traveler has been sipping water
From his cupped hand,
Keeping his fingers wide apart,
All the while looking up towards the woman at the well,
Who in turn has reduced the already thin stream
To a mere trickle.   [161]

517

After the flicker of a side glance
From the daughter-in-law
The traveler, refused entry
By the master of the house,
Spent the night on the veranda.   [254]

518

Mother, if you ask me what made me cry,
It's that traveler dozing in our courtyard
Who in his dream pleaded: "Stop being angry,
Please stop being angry and turn over."   [807]

519

See how the winter traveler
At the gate of the village temple

Jabs at the smoldering heap of husks
As if it were a bear. [109]

520

Covered all over with gooseflesh,
Visibly shivering,
Sucking in his breath between clenched teeth:
The winter wayfarer
Looks like a man making love. [721]

521

The spring wind stirs the forest,
Loud with the drone of bees,
And the cowgirl's song
About parted lovers
Troubles the lonely traveler. [128]

522

In despair
The travelers stare at the new shoot on the mango tree,
As though it were one of Love's arrows
Crimson with a clot of blood. [586]

523

Cautiously,
As if it were a matter of high treason,
One traveler said to the other:
"There are shoots on the mango trees.
So it can't be long now." [396]

524

In the midday heat of summer
The mere thought of the refreshing stream of cool moonlight

From his wife's round face
Restores the traveler. [399]

525

Wayfarer,
Your shadow is hiding beneath your body,
Not showing one bit of itself for fear of the midday sun,
So why don't you too take a rest? [49]

526

However abundant,
A miser's wealth is useless,
Like the traveler's shadow
When he is scorched by the summer heat. [136]

527

Laughing and clapping,
The travelers run towards the shady banyan
Loaded with juicy fruit
When a flock of parrots flies up
To reveal a bare, shrivelled tree. [263]

528

At the approach of the rains
The traveler is so intent on getting home
That he bundles up the road and takes it with him,
That he cuts it into manageable pieces,
That he swallows it down in one gulp. [696]

529

Cloud,
Thunder with all your might above me,

For I have a heart of iron.
But spare my poor girl at home,
Who has already loosened her hair,
As it would be death to her. [567]

530

Aunt,
As the traveler hastens homewards,
His business unfinished,
The start of the rainy season,
With its white *kuṭaja* flowers,
Seems to mock him with loud laughter. [538]

531

Look how the traveler thrills
As he sniffs at the sweetwood flower,
Caresses it, kisses it,
And presses it against his heart
As if it were his wife's pale cheek. [641]

532

Sniffing the wayside *kadamba* blossom,
Your eyes full of tears,
Take heart, young traveler!
You are sure to see the face of your wife again. [566]

533

Hey, you fool,
Can't you walk a little faster?
The poor girl is dying.
Stop dragging your feet.
The mere sight of you will revive her.
No doubt of it. [588]

534

The lie of the land is blurred
And everywhere progress gets slower:
Soon the roads will be impassable
Even for the wheels of his fancy.   [675]

535

He was so distracted with worry
About his wife not surviving the long separation
That, reaching his house,
He walked on.   [707]

COUNTRY CHARACTERS

Throughout the anthology village is contrasted with town. What town girls do out of sophistication village girls do out of simplicity (536, 537). Even so, life among the village yokels is dull—certainly for someone accustomed to more congenial company and greater comfort (540).

The countryside is peopled by petty farmers, hunters, cowherds, and their like. Beside these there is a rural elite consisting of the landowner, the village headman and the tax gatherer. The farmer is poor and cannot afford precious ornaments for his wife, but fortunately she is unspoilt and joyfully sports the pair of berries he gives her as a love token behind her ear (541). Hard work in the fields leaves him little time or energy for love, and anyway things are apt to go wrong: as he sows, he dreams of making love in the ripening crop and gets so excited that the seeds stick to his sweaty palm (544); when autumn at last offers a lull in his toil, the bright, moonlit nights are unsuitable for secret trysts (548). The farmer's wife is no better: when she has to paint an auspicious sign on the plowshare at the start of the plowing season, her hand trembles so much at the thought of making love in the field of cotton that she cannot proceed (545).

In his dealings with the upper echelons of village society, such as the tax gatherer's wife or the landowner, the peasant betrays his primitive manners. Poem 558 describes the unsubtle way in which a farmer's daughter tries to attract the notice of her husband, the son of a wealthy landowner.

The headman is completely taken up with his work of protecting the village and has no time for flirting. The disappointed girls liken him to a worm in a *neem* fruit, which most people find too bitter to eat (561). His chest is so rough with scars that his poor wife finds it hard to rest her face on it (560).

A character comparable to the fierce headman is the wrestler. Like the headman he looks forbidding (564), while his victories are won at the cost of neglecting his wife (565).

Despite his appearance, the headman is a person of some importance in the village. On his deathbed, he solemnly urges his son to be worthy of the family name but unfortunately makes a hash of his dying injunction (563). His funeral also turns into a fiasco when his wife, passionately embracing his dead body on the pyre, so far forgets herself as to break into a sweat which puts out the fire (568). The dramatic spectacle of the funeral, where all his wives line up to join him on the pyre, turns awkward when the corpse's eyes seem to be fixed on his favorite wife. Even in death . . . (569).

The Pulindas are tribal hunters who live in the Vindhya hills. In the poems they are a byword for foolishness. For example, they string their bows at the sight of rain clouds, mistaking them for elephants (573).

The poems about the hunter focus mainly on the incompatibility of his calling with a happy marriage. He is so exhausted by making love to his wife that he can no longer draw his stout bow and has to shave it thinner each day (577). As a result big game eludes him, and he has to turn to easier targets such as peacocks. The peacock feathers worn by his young wife are a token of his love, but the pearls worn by his other, less-favored wives are a reminder that once he had the strength to kill elephants (whose foreheads are thought to secrete pearls) (583). Worse still, his new love seems to have made him sentimental: he can no longer bring himself to kill deer, who form faithful attachments (584).

536

> Village girls with swelling bosoms
> Need only simple saffron yellow blouses
> To attract the most sophisticated of lovers.   [546]

537

I was born and raised in a village,
I live in a village,
And with the ways of the town
I am not familiar.
Still,
I attract the husbands of the women in town.
I am what I am. [705]

538

Little girl,
You can still play bunny hops
But don't go walking around naked:
The youths of the village
Know the mother by the daughter. [741]

539

Blind with love
I threw my arms around him,
Taking him for a farmer's boy.
But when I touched him
He was just a spiky scarecrow
At the village boundary. [751]

540

To whom can I give a sly glance,
With whom can I share my joys and sorrows,
With whom can I joke,
In this dump of a village
Full of yokels? [164]

541

Delighted with the modest pair of berries you gave her,
Your wife, though usually so shy, has gone home

Down the center of the village street,
Wearing them behind her ear. [419]

542

The plowman's son in this damned village
Hasn't a clue.
The landowner's daughter is dying
But with no doctor at hand
Whom to tell? [602]

543

When he fell asleep,
Exhausted after a day of dragging the plow through
    thick mud,
His wife,
Angry at missing the pleasures of love,
Cursed the rainy season. [324]

544

As he sows,
The seeds stick to the farmer's hands
Which grow moist
When he thinks that soon he might be making love
With his girl in this very field. [358]

545

As the faithless wife puts the auspicious mark on the
    plowshare
On the first day of plowing the cotton field
She is already so full of desire that her hands tremble. [165]

546

When the plowman took to flight,
Fearing the good lady was dead

When she had only swooned in love's ecstasy,
The cotton plant, bowed under its white, half-opened pods,
Seemed to smile. [360]

547

Look!
The landowner's son has already plucked the cotton
But his simple wife lingers, vainly stroking the empty pods
With a trembling and sweaty hand. [359]

548

In autumn, when the corn is ripe,
The farmer would do as he likes
If only the moonlit nights weren't bright
As the fresh grains of husked rice. [691]

549

To desert the lotus
For the scent of ripe wood-apple—
As soon as you touch it, silly bee,
You'll find out your mistake,
Like the yokel
Who reached for a sweetmeat in a painting. [643]

550

When at dawn he sees a long swathe of green
Through the frost-white field of sesame
—His faithless wife's clandestine trail—
The farmer blames himself for letting loose the bulls. [695]

551

Seeing his wife's dark breasts
Which, but for the absence of smoke,

Resemble black heaps of burning chaff,
The farmer barters his cloak for a buffalo
In the cold month of Māgha.   [238]

552

Who needs a blanket,
Who needs a fire,
And who needs a bedchamber,
If he has a wife with warm breasts
Lying snug against his chest?   [772]

553

In winter one can recognize a poor man
By his tattered, threadbare clothes
Reeking of cow-dung fires and brown with smoke.   [329]

554

After she who peeped in to ask how he was
Had with her fragrant breath
Cooled the bitter medicine,
The plowman drained it to the very last drop.   [317]

555

Lovely woman,
The farmer has become so thin
On your account
That his good wife, though jealous,
Now acts as go-between.   [84]

556

Though he had no more work in the fields,
The farmer would not go home,

To spare himself the pain
Of finding it empty
Now his wife was dead. [169]

557

In the house left empty by his wife's death
The plowman is consumed by grief,
Staring at where they used to make love
As though at hiding places robbed of their treasure. [373]

558

When the poor plowman's daughter
Saw her courteous husband standing on the river bank
She clambered up
By the most difficult route. [107]

559

The plowman is so spoilt by the sweets
The tax gatherer's wife has given him to eat
That he now turns up his nose at all other sweets. [605]

560

Lying on his breast,
Rough with the scars of many a wound,
The headman's wife finds it difficult to rest,
But his village sleeps sound. [31]

561

Headman's son,
How heartless you are!
Shying away from your wife
You rarely show yourself,

Like a worm in a *neem* berry.
Yet because of you
The whole village is pining away.   [30]

562

As his relatives suspected
And his enemies feared,
The headman's son,
Though still very young,
Has proved excellent
At protecting the village.   [630]

563

On his deathbed
The headman of the hamlet
Earnestly instructs his son:
"Act in such a way
As not to be ashamed of my name."   [634]

564

The old wrestler
With ears mangled by many a fight
Has only to gird up his loins
For his fearful opponent to lose heart.   [686]

565

Instead of dancing for joy
Should you not feel shame?
The drum that celebrates your husband's victory
In the wrestling match
Makes your unhappy marriage
Known to all the world.   [687]

566

The village headman's daughter is such a beauty
That she has on her own turned all the men of the village
    into gods
By making them unable to blink. [593]

567

Though still a child,
The village headman's daughter
Already turns everybody's head.
Once she is grown up
She will cause real harm,
Like a poisonous creeper. [410]

568

Her body
Sweating with the pleasure
Of tightly embracing her beloved husband,
The landowner's daughter
Puts out the flames of his pyre. [407]

569

All the village headman's wives
Are dressed in readiness to follow him on the pyre,
Yet even at this heartrending moment
His eyes fall upon his favorite. [449]

570

As the good wife prepared
To join her beloved on the pyre
He came back to life,
And her widow's finery
Turned to that of married bliss. [635]

571

Look!
While the cowherd is chatting up the maid
His young wife angrily sets all the calves free. [731]

572

People are not captivated by true qualities
But by what takes their fancy.
The Pulindas brush pearls aside
But seize upon the *guñja* seeds
The jeweler uses as weights. [310]

573

On the heights of the Vindhya
The Pulindas kneel behind their bows
The moment they see the valleys below
Filling with rain clouds
As if with a herd of elephants. [116]

574

When the Pulinda hunter's wife
Saw her husband's lip
Swollen by a bee sting,
She was stung herself
By jealousy
And fled
To stand in the shade of another tree. [636]

575

Though completely exhausted by making love to his
    young wife,
He did not wish to hurt the feelings of his elder wife.

So the hunter took his bow with him into the forest
Even though he could not bend it
Without first shaving it thinner. [122]

576

See how the wood shavings
Swirl above the hunter's homestead,
Like a banner
Announcing the joys of marriage. [120]

577

For how many days
Has the hunter's young and beautiful wife
Proudly scattered her happiness all over the streets
In the guise of shavings from her husband's bow? [119]

578

When our hunter
In the middle of the village, for everybody to see,
Started to cut sections into his gruesome bow
Mother-in-law began to cry
Louder even than on the day her husband died. [665]

579

The fuller the breasts of the hunter's wife
The thinner her waist,
The thinner her loving husband and his bow,
The thinner the youths in her village,
And the thinner her husband's other wives. [598]

580

That daughter-in-law has turned our son
Into a trembling wreck:

Once he needed just one arrow
To make an elephant cow a widow,
Now he carries a quiverful. [632]

581

The breasts of the huntsman's wife rise
As if to tell the elephant, rhinoceros and ox,
The deer, buffalo, tiger and bear
That from her husband
They have nothing to fear. [742]

582

Merchant,
How are we to supply elephant tusks
And tiger skins
While my daughter-in-law walks about the house
Waggling her bottom
And with her hair hanging loose around her face? [951]

583

With a tame peacock's tail feather behind her ear
The hunter's young wife saunters among his elder wives
Who are themselves decked out with pearls
Which their husband once cut loose
From the temples of fierce elephants. [173]

584

The doe looked at the solitary stag
With such longing
That the bow dropped from the hand
Of the hunter
Whose wife was dear to him. [620]

585

Trader,
For hides of the spotted deer
You'll have to go elsewhere.
Our young hunter
No longer bends his bow
To shoot deer.   [631]

586

As the stag steps in front of the doe
To face the arrow
And then the doe steps in front of the stag,
The hunter throws away his bow
Drenched with tears of distress.   [603]

587

Mortally wounded by a sharp arrow
Shot from behind the hunter's ear,
The doe, knowing she would not see her mate again,
Rolled over and fixed him with a lingering gaze.   [595]

GODS AND SAINTS

As far as their love lives are concerned the gods are subject to the same emotions and complications as ordinary men. When Śiva offers a handful of water to Twilight, he makes his wife, Pārvatī/Gaurī, jealous (591). When Pārvatī wants to cover Śiva's three eyes to prevent him from seeing her naked, she finds herself one hand short (589).

The mythology of the cowherd god Kṛṣṇa mainly revolves around his erotic escapades with the cowgirls from Vraja. When his mother, Yaśodā, tells them that he is still only a child, they know better (592). Poem 594 describes how the cowgirls compete for Kṛṣṇa's attention with Rādhā, his favorite.

Several poems in the anthology allude to the primordial churning of the Ocean of Milk (e.g., 588). Both gods and demons churned the ocean to obtain the drink of immortality, each side pulling at one end of the rope which makes the dasher spin round. The demons won but were tricked into handing over the drink to the gods by Viṣṇu disguised as a beautiful girl.

Like the gods, monks and ascetics are not impervious to female beauty. Mendicant monks, who go begging from door to door, have ample opportunity for encounters with women (595). As part of their ascetic practices *kāpālika* monks wear garlands of skulls and smear their bodies with the ashes from funeral pyres. The nun in poem 597 gets so excited by daubing herself with the ash from her lover's funeral pyre that she breaks into a sweat, which washes it off again.

588

That they are churning the ocean
To retrieve the nectar of immortality
Only shows that the gods have not yet tasted
   your lips. [594]

589

Long live Śiva's third eye
Which Pārvatī covered with kisses
While covering his other two eyes with her hands
When her skirt slipped off in the heat of love play. [455]

590

Already at her wedding
Pārvatī's friends knew she would be happy
When Śiva tossed aside
The snake bracelet that frightened her. [69]

591

Bow before Śiva's offering to Twilight,
The water held in his cupped hand.
Reflecting Gaurī's moonlike face,
Now flushed with jealous anger,
It looks more like a crimson lotus. [1]

592

As his mother Yaśodā says:
"Kṛṣṇa is still a child,"
The women of Vraja smile to themselves,
Their eyes fixed on his face. [112]

593

When Kṛṣṇa came of age
And the time of his marriage drew near

The young cowgirls tried to conceal their family ties
With his mother Yaśodā. [657]

594

Placing herself next to Rādhā
On the pretext of praising the way she dances,
The cunning cowgirl manages to kiss Kṛṣṇa,
Who is reflected in his favorite's cheek. [114]

595

While the begging monk looks down at her navel,
And the housewife looks at the moon of his face,
The crows plunder the dish in her hands
And the begging bowl in his. [162]

596

The pain inflicted by the sidelong glances
Of seductive women
—Saints suffer it too
But they master their emotions. [817]

597

The *kāpālika* novice cannot stop daubing her body
With ashes that come from her lover's pyre:
The pleasure of touching them
Brings her out in a sweat. [408]

THE GOD OF LOVE

The Indian God of Love, Kāma, is said to be bodiless. He exists only in people's minds, and so do his arrows. Which is why they do not wound, yet cause terrible pain (599). The arrows are like flowers, the sight of which makes one think of love (602). Spring has the same effect and is therefore said to be the God of Love's domain and hunting ground (608).

598

How very puzzling!
Though made of flowers
They are extremely sharp.
Though they make no contact
They are irresistibly powerful.
Though they cut through the flesh
They cause delight
—The arrows of the God of Love.   [326]

599

They pierce one's body,
Cause pain
But without making wounds.
Ah! Love's arrows are unique.   [748]

600

They cause jealousy,
Kindle love,

Make grief bearable
And prevent separation from being fatal:
Love's arrows have so many different effects. [327]

601

They cause grief,
Give pleasure,
Create a longing
And allay it:
Praised be the arrows of the God of Love,
Kindred of pleasure and pain. [325]

602

Friend,
The orange *kadamba* flowers give me more pain
Than all other flowers put together.
It's as if these days
The God of Love has a bow that shoots sweets. [177]

603

Friend,
Whoever it was who sang this song
So early in the morning,
He must have been thinking of some lover,
For he reopened the wounds
That the God of Love had made in my heart
With his sharp arrows. [381]

604

Even in my next existence,
O God of Love,
I will dedicate my life
In worship at your feet,

If you promise to pierce him
With the same arrow
As you pierced me with.   [441]

605

Try though she would to keep it,
The advice given by her friends
Escaped from her heart
That was shattered by the arrow of the God of Love.   [101]

606

Returning from the late afternoon bath,
Their eyes red
And their buttocks visible through wet skirts
—Love need not carry a bow
On behalf of these women.   [473]

607

The drowsy glances of a moon-faced woman,
Her half-veiled pupils darting to and fro,
Are irresistible
Even to the God of Love.   [148]

608

Spring offers her body
With its drifting fragrance,
Leafspray fingers,
And cloak of tender flowers
As a playground
To the God of Love.   [782]

609

Friend,
The wretched fire of love

Is an odd sort of fire:
In a sapless heart it goes out,
In a sappy one it instantly flares up.   [430]

ALLEGORICAL VERSES

The bee, which roams from one flower to the next, offers an ideal object of comparison with the fickle lover. Its frantic and impatient attempts to penetrate the flower and get at the nectar resemble the act of making love. A number of poems by describing the bee suggest the lover. In others the bee is not described but spoken to. In poem 610 a woman tells the bee that if he wants the jasmine's nectar he will have to work harder and in poem 615 that it is heartless to forsake a plant once it bears fruit. In both poems the message is clearly intended to be overheard by the lover.

Another characteristic of the bee, and of other animals too, is that it is easily fooled by resemblances. When a girl puts her pink foot, heel down and toes up, into the sluice to block the flow of water into the paddy field, the bees, mistaking it for a lotus, circle around it (621). Likewise they hover around a girl's face, which resembles a lotus except that it does not close at night (622). The doe (626), the elephant (633) and the monkey (635) all suffer from similar delusions as the bee. The doe and stag are held up as an example of selfless love (628).

610

O bee,
To get at the jasmine's nectar
You have to knead and squeeze long and hard.
It does not open by itself.   [444]

611

Eager to taste the fresh nectar
That seeps from between the petals
At the moment they unfold,
There is nothing the bee will not do
To the jasmine's closed bud. [591]

612

The bee is so eager to taste the fresh nectar,
He cannot stop to unfold the tight-knit petals
But simply pierces the tip of the bud. [615]

613

Aunt,
There must be something very special about the early
    jasmine
That we don't know about,
Such that all the bees converge on its tiny flowers. [592]

614

Bees settle on it,
Buzzing wildly,
Lusting for its sweet nectar
But the lotus opens
Only after being kissed by the sun. [495]

615

Ungrateful bee,
Once you would not think
Of enjoying yourself with other flowers
But now that the jasmine is heavy with fruit
You forsake her. [92]

616

That the bee wants to drink the nectar
Of one flower after another
Is the fault of the flowers running out of nectar,
Not the bee's. [139]

617

Bee,
Only were you to find in another flower
As much nectar as you find inside the pollen-filled lotus
Would you be right to hover around it. [387]

618

O bee,
One moment you hover above the lotuses,
The next you brush against the mimosa,
Then you stay glued to the jasmine.
Perhaps the trumpetflowers will cure you
Of this fickleness. [621]

619

Do you know, my daughter,
What the poor bee did
In the absence of the jasmine flower?
He threw himself into the red *aśoka* flowers
As into a fire. [754]

620

One moment the bees are hovering
Over the bright fingernails
Of the girl picking flowers,
The next over the flowers,

The next over the shoots,
And the next over the girl's hands.   [796]

621

Bees circle round the rice girl's pink foot
Placed across the sluice
To stop the water flowing
Into the paddy field.   [692]

622

Attracted by her fragrant breath,
Bees cluster round her face
That is like no other lotus
Since the moon cannot outshine it.   [366]

623

A swarm of bees blindly pursues the parrot
Whose feathers are spattered with the juice
Dripping from the mango it has pecked with its beak.   [668]

624

Not without reason
Do the bees hover eagerly
Over the grove of mangoes.
There is no smoke without fire.   [544]

625

Though the twigs were completely bare,
The bees clung to the jasmine,
Savoring the memory of the scent
Which burst from the buds that had been there.   [755]

626

While all around the forest is burning,
Lines of red flame steadily advancing,
The foolish doe does not flee,
Imagining herself in a forest of flame trees.   [589]

627

The stag thought that she was more thirsty than he
And the doe thought that he was more thirsty than she.
In this way the thirsty couple
Out of consideration for each other
Did not drink at all!   [763]

628

In the jungle grass and water
Are everywhere free for the asking,
And still the love between a doe and a stag
Lasts until death.   [287]

629

Fettered by affection
The she-elephant circles around in distress
And stretches out her trunk to rescue
Her husband who is stuck in the mud.   [454]

630

Though tormented with hunger
The elephant allows the tasty mouthful of lotus roots
In his trunk
To dry up and wither
As he stands thinking of the face of his favorite wife.   [383]

631

How can an elephant
Ever become leader of the herd
If he leaves the Vindhya
With its wild rice
For the sake of a mouthful of rice
From a paddy field?   [788]

632

Soiled with dust,
Spattered with mud
And nourished with grass,
Yet, on account of his size,
It is the elephant who carries the big drum.   [527]

633

See how the elephant tries in vain
To wet its head beneath a snake's sloughed skin
That hangs down from a rocky sill,
Mistaking it for a waterfall.   [642]

634

Parched by the heat, the buffalo licks a snake,
Taking it for a mountain rivulet,
And the snake sips the buffalo's spittle,
Taking it for water falling from black rock.   [552]

635

The monkey scratches the rose apple with its finger,
Jumps away, shakes the branch, screeching loudly,
But does not dare to pluck it
As it looks like the bee
That once stung him.   [532]

POETIC FANCY

Most of the poems in the anthology are in the form of monologues, and many have a conversational tone. At the same time they are rich in figures of speech, ranging from simple comparisons to complex images. A monologue may take the form of a comparison, as when someone observes that the only thing that remotely matches a certain woman's right half is her left half (636). Some comparisons belong to the standard repertory of Indian poetry. For instance, the comparison of a woman's face with the moon (639) or a lotus (642) and of her smooth cheeks with a mirror (644). There are verses where one comparison is piled on top of another (649) or where the words used to describe the properties common to the two things compared have double meanings. This is the case with poem 651, in which a woman's breasts are compared to a good poem. A further example is 648, where people stare in admiration at a village girl who gets powdered with flour as she grinds grain. Each part of the scene has a counterpart in the scene it is compared with: the people staring are compared to gods, who are believed never to blink, the girl powdered with flour to the Goddess Lakṣmī as she arose from the Ocean of Milk spattered with milk.

A particularly striking image can be a poem's whole purpose. In some cases it may be possible to detect an erotic allusion (658) but usually such a connection is far-fetched. Poem 665 is basically a fanciful description of a downpour, with the cloud pictured as groaning with the effort of trying to lift the earth with its ropes of raindrops. While rain, or rather the rainy season, plays an important role in the love lives of the wayfarer and his wife, this poem does not seem to have any erotic connotations. As with the other poems in this section, it displays the exuberance of poetic fancy.

636

In the whole wide world
Teeming with thousands of beautiful women
The only thing that matches this woman's right side . . .
Is her left side.   [303]

637

Long-lashed, dazzling white, black and slanting
— There are plenty of other women with eyes like that
But that does not mean they know how to look.   [470]

638

O, *aśoka* tree,
There is nothing more for you to achieve:
Your leaves have been compared to the hand of a lovely
    woman.   [404]

639

Daughter, be warned:
It's a new moon.
So do not sleep in the courtyard tonight
Lest the moon-eating demon swallow your face by
    mistake.   [804]

640

Every time the moon is full
The Creator takes it apart again

To refashion it in such a way
That it might match your face. [207]

641

Handsome man,
If you want to enjoy the sight
Of every phase of the moon
Look at her gentle face
As she slowly lifts her bodice
Over her head. [674]

642

Lovely woman,
Don't cover your face with your shawl.
Let the sun find out which is more pleasant to touch,
Your face
Or the lotus. [269]

643

Reflected in the deer-eyed woman's cheek
Covered with fresh tooth marks,
The moon looks like a white conch shell
Red on the inside. [300]

644

How surprised the girl is
To see her friend's cheek in the mirror
And the mirror in her cheek. [824]

645

If her eyes were not closed
In ecstasy

At seeing her lover,
Who would notice the blue lily
Behind her ear? [323]

646

The line of bees around the large lotus flower,
Feasting loudly on its nectar,
Looks like the jingling girdle of sapphires
Around the waist of the nymph of spring. [575]

647

Drunken bees sit motionless
On the petals of the white lotus
Like specks of darkness
Forgotten by the rays of the moon. [562]

648

Full of desire, the passers-by halt
And stare at the plowman's daughter
Who is powdered with flour,
Without blinking their eyes,
As if they were the gods
And she the goddess Lakṣmī
Rising up from the Ocean of Milk. [388]

649

Like a house without furnishings,
Like the basin of a waterfall without water,
Like a cowshed without cattle
—Her face without you. [611]

650

The girl's thick, fragrant hair
Is like a column of smoke rising from the fire of love,

Like a bunch of peacock's tail feathers
Waved by the conjuror to distract his audience,
Like the victory banner of youth. [573]

651

Who is not captivated by a woman's breasts,
That, like a good poem,
Are a pleasure to grasp,
Are weighty, compact, and nicely ornamented? [428]

652

With cooing doves hidden high up among the rafters
The temple groans like a man suffering from cramp. [64]

653

In the rainy season
The peacock,
Stretching its long neck,
Pecks at the raindrop
That hangs on the tip of a grass blade
Like a pearl pierced by an emerald needle. [394]

654

With great difficulty
Birds find a place to rest
In the treetops,
Fluttering their wings
And shifting their feet
At the tips of the dark branches
That bend beneath their weight. [662]

655

Look at that heron
Standing absolutely motionless

On the lotus leaf.
It is just like mother of pearl
In a setting of spotless emerald.   [4]

656

Look at the flock of parrots
Flying out of the hole in that tree
As though it had an autumn fever
And were spitting blood and bile.   [563]

657

Look!
A flock of parrots falling from the sky
Like a necklace of rubies and emeralds
Slipping from the throat of Śrī in heaven.   [75]

658

Look!
A tender shoot has sprouted from the stone of a ripe mango.
It looks like an eel hiding in a half-opened oyster shell.   [62]

659

Look at that spider climbing down from the rafters
Along a thread spun from between its feet:
It looks like a mimosa flower strung on an invisible
    string.   [63]

660

With clouds torn to shreds
And dispersed in all directions
—A few still sticking to its slopes—
The Vindhya Range seems to shed its skin.   [115]

661

The Vindhya Range with white clouds
Clinging to its body blackened by forest fires
Looks like Viṣṇu splashed
While churning the Ocean of Milk.   [117]

662

Summer reveals what was never seen before:
The bottom of the pond
With turtles and minnows
Struggling in the thick, dry mud and heat.   [414]

663

With a dry crust of mud on the surface
But still wet below
The village streets seem to sigh heavily
As people go to and fro.   [625]

664

After burning the entire forest
The fire was worn out
With crossing hill and plain.
So, holding on to the grass that grew on the steep bank,
It went down to the river for a drink.   [758]

665

Hear how that cloud groans with the effort,
Yet is unable to lift the earth
With ropes of raindrops
That fall in unbroken streams.   [436]

666

Unable to grip the new blade of grass
With its teeth or lips,

The cow merely licks it with its tongue
As one does a bruised lip. [801]

667

A swarm of gnats hovers over the buffalo's shoulders.
When he hits them with his horn
They hum like the plucked strings of a lute. [561]

668

The crows on the boundary fence,
With their faces bedraggled, their wings drooping, their
    necks sunken,
Look as though they had been impaled. [564]

669

The flowers of the flame trees,
Which resemble parrots' beaks,
Make the ground resplendent,
Like a congregation of monks
Prostrate in worship at the feet
Of the Buddha. [308]

670

At noon in summer
The trees in the deserted forest,
Scorched by the unbearable rays of the sun,
Seem to cry out with the shrill creak
Of crickets. [494]

671

In summer the rattle of the grindstone
Makes it seem that the houses are snoring
While the doors, their eyes, remain shut
And the servants make no stir inside. [800]

GOOD MEN AND BAD

The good man defined in the following poems is not the counterpart of the perfect wife. He is what might be called a real gentleman, a man who is reliable (679), does not betray his emotions (673) and who is won over only by goodness (687). However rare, such men do exist (678). But this does not mean that goodness is an absolute virtue: what is good for one person need not be good for another (685).

672

The hearts of good men are like the tops of tall trees:
When laden with fruit
They are bent on sharing
And when bare they are uplifted. [282]

673

A lake in autumn
Is warm only on the surface.
Below it stays cool,
Like a good man when displeased. [186]

674

A gentleman never gets angry.
When he gets angry

He never has nasty thoughts.
When he has nasty thoughts
He never expresses them.
When he expresses them
He is ashamed of himself.   [250]

675

What has the hot sun,
Which makes the lotuses unfold,
In common with the cool moon
Which makes the water lilies unfold?
It's as with a good man's affection,
Which does not alter
However far away he may be.   [753]

676

I'd rather have something in between.
For what use is a bad man
Or, for that matter, a good one?
A bad man causes pain by his presence,
A good man by his absence.   [224]

677

Dealings with sympathetic people,
Even if inconclusive,
Are, I think, more pleasant
Than dealings concluded
With their opposite.   [61]

678

In this damned world of ours, so full of crooks,
A decent man is rarely seen.
The earth teems with crows
But geese are few and far between.   [710]

679

Like writing on water
Friendship with a bad man
Fades as soon as it's begun.
With a good man it is immutable
Like an inscription in stone. [272]

680

Make a friend of the man
Who, wherever or whenever it may be,
Stands by you in adversity
Steady as an image in a wall painting. [217]

681

The bow shoots the arrow
The moment it touches the string.
How long can straight and crooked stay together? [424]

682

When full of water, they swing high.
When empty, they lie low for a while.
—The buckets on a water wheel
Behave just like nasty people. [490]

683

Happy are the deaf and the blind!
Though they live among humankind
They hear not a single word of slander
Nor see how the wicked prosper. [704]

684

The fire that burns in the outcast's hut
Then burns on the sacrificial altar.

Never shun a person
However wretched his circumstances. [227]

685

Winter,
Which is cool for people
Wilts the lotuses.
How can we truly know the world
When it varies according to circumstance? [773]

686

Lotuses know that winter is hot
Because it makes them wilt.
However much they try to hide their true nature,
People are betrayed by their acts. [730]

687

A man who knows the ultimate truth
Is only won over by true goodness,
For who can trick an old cat with rice gruel? [286]

EPILOGUE

In old age one's hair turns gray and one's breasts, those veterans of the battle of love, sag (692, 693). The scars of old nail marks look like the traces of a temple of the God of Love (691). The bowers, which were the trysting places of the lovers when young, are now bare stumps (698). With old age love vanishes and with it the desire and the daring to have an affair (701). All one is left with are memories and regrets (700).

688

There were the young men,
The blessings of village life,
And the days of our youth.
Now people make a story of it,
And we listen. [518]

689

Of a couple,
Who after a long life of shared joys and sorrows
Have learned the meaning of love,
The one who dies survives,
The other is as good as dead. [142]

690

Don't worry, dear girl,
When youth and beauty are all but gone

You can still cause pain,
Like the sight of one's birthplace
From which the familiar faces
Have vanished. [340]

691

The nail marks on the breasts, thighs and buttocks
Of beauties past their prime
Resemble the traces of an abandoned temple
Of the God of Love. [233]

692

After the rainy season
With towering clouds,
Like youth with plump breasts,
Has spent itself,
Plumes of *kāśa* grass,
Like the first strands of gray hair,
Appear on Mother Earth. [434]

693

Prominent and pressing close,
Decorated with fresh scars, their duty done,
Like two warriors, a woman's breasts
Are handsome even as they collapse. [427]

694

Thinking how wretched it is
To be sagging over her stomach
After having once been prominent
—That's how her breasts must have got dark nipples. [83]

695

How come that her breasts,
Once so firm,

Now sag like this?
On the other hand,
Who abides forever in a woman's heart? [268]

696

Fallen from our former position,
Our abundance wasted away,
No longer prominent,
We stare at our navels
Like an old woman's breasts. [654]

697

The friends of our youth have passed away,
Of those bowers nothing remains but stumps,
Gone is the vigor of former days,
And love has been cut to the roots. [232]

698

Remember those *vañjula* trees on the riverbank
Whose blossom was bowed by clusters of bees?
Time, dear friend, has turned them to stumps. [422]

699

Though I am nearing death,
I swear that, even now,
My gaze falls, as ever,
On the thicket that grows
By the banks of the holy Taptī. [239]

700

Impossible, even for a moment,
To banish her dark presence from my heart.

Every day the same pain, undiminished,
Like being haunted by a secret sin. [183]

701

Oh! the passage of time:
This young man,
Weary of passionate poems,
Now studies law
While we . . .
We stick to our husbands. [892]

VARIANT READINGS

2 [2] *taṃtatattiṃ,* **98** [768] *ajjaṃ kallaṃ va,* **166** [651] *jai jaṃpai jaṇo vi,* **202** [759] *paṃḍiaittaṃ* (?), **220** [949] *kaaveṇiāṇa,* **334** [488] *āṇāvarāhe, pesattaṇāvarāhe,* **343** [188] *māṇapauttthaṃ,* **353** [420] *paravasaṇaṇaccirīhiṃ,* **369** [33] *ālimgasi kīsa maṃ parāhuttiṃ,* **372** [26] *kuṇaṃti ccia, jāṇaṃtī,* **384** [943] *ṇa daṃsase piṭṭhaṃ,* **387** [226] *pāaṃtasuttāe,* **412** [550] *phalahī,* **428** [54] *sirivaṃdīṇaṃ,* **494** [539] *oraṃtamuhīe,* **500** [437] *atthakkāaavīsaṃbhaghāi,* **503** [76] *āsaṃghia,* **522** [586] *lohiuppakka,* **535** [707] *āsaṃghiavasahī,* **580** [632] *viṇaḍio,* **594** [114] *sirigoviāe,* **599** [748] *ṇeya tāṇaṃ khayamaggo* (?), **606** [473] *kae ṇa,* **608** [782] *aṃgaṃ chittaṃ (chettaṃ) piva vammahassa,* **621** [692] *ahilijjai,* **631** [788] *vaṇasāliṇo.*

205

CONCORDANCE OF VERSES IN WEBER'S EDITION AND THIS TRANSLATION

1=591 2=2 3=1 4=655 5=239 8=235 9=65 10=97 11=396 13=174
14=173 15=253 16=469 17=312 19=104 20=79 21=50 22=215 23=151
24=299 26=372 27=374 28=191 29=486 30=561 31=560 32=311
33=369 35=260 36=445 38=254 39=504 40=118 41=106 42=430
43=126 44=278 45=361 46=80 47=434 48=277 49=525 50=294
51=295 52=207 53=397 54=428 55=427 56=234 58=441 59=257
60=368 61=677 62=658 63=659 64=652 65=81 66=420 67=45
68=242 69=590 70=485 71=363 72=113 73=162 74=391 75=657
76=503 78=186 79=274 80=51 81=122 83=694 84=555 85=296
86=394 87=377 88=318 90=332 91=344 92=615 93=27 95=107
96=83 97=478 98=247 99=109 100=229

101=605 103=63 104=64 105=99 106=270 107=558 108=342
109=519 110=236 111=437 112=592 114=594 115=660 116=573
117=661 118=425 119=577 120=576 122=575 123=273 124=465
125=159 126=284 127=201 128=521 130=256 132=123 133=462
134=136 136=526 137=502 139=616 140=497 141=116 142=689
143=431 144=320 145=231 146=290 148=607 150=232 152=365
153=448 154=103 155=241 156=203 157=117 158=86 159=417 160=352
161=516 162=595 163=340 164=540 165=545 166=413 168=48
169=556 170=491 173=583 174=108 175=62 176=188 177=602
178=134 179=350 180=303 181=132 182=288 183=700 184=379

185=450 186=673 187=52 188=343 189=42 190=440 192=219
193=44 194=499 195=337 196=206 197=419 198=128 199=22
200=228

201=96 202=102 203=280 205=463 206=501 207=640 208=443
209=150 210=29 211=195 212=271 213=185 214=49 215=382 216=347
217=680 218=56 219=408 220=4 221=5 222=449 223=23 224=676
225=25 226=387 227=684 228=399 229=40 231=68 232=697
233=691 234=161 235=167 236=121 237=402 238=551 239=699
240=282 244=471 246=43 247=362 249=69 250=674 252=78
254=517 256=496 257=6 258=10 260=12 261=429 262=498
263=527 268=695 269=642 270=393 271=160 272=679 273=508
274=196 275=285 276=180 277=333 280=326 281=268 282=672
283=464 286=687 287=628 288=179 289=218 290=255 291=405
292=267 293=251 294=144 295=414 296=141 297=401 298=140
299=244 300=643

302=325 303=636 304=115 305=110 306=351 307=447 308=669
309=364 310=572 312=35 313=410 314=163 315=490 317=554 318=54
322=477 323=645 324=543 325=601 326=598 327=600 328=34
329=553 331=424 333=193 335=444 336=489 337=286 338=24
339=452 340=690 341=31 343=142 344=178 345=105 347=293
348=89 349=467 350=281 351=158 352=90 353=298 354=367 355=61
357=93 358=544 359=547 360=546 361=168 363=473 365=53
366=622 367=21 368=371 369=37 370=19 371=20 373=557 374=373
375=339 376=381 377=91 378=165 379=514 381=603 382=266
383=630 384=385 385=77 386=488 387=617 388=648 389=92
390=346 391=210 392=192 393=30 394=653 395=13 396=523
397=454 399=524 400=194

401=338 404=638 407=568 408=597 409=227 410=567 412=476
413=246 414=662 415=75 416=67 417=404 418=169 419=541
420=353 422=698 423=124 424=681 426=330 427=693 428=651
429=182 430=609 431=358 432=359 433=233 434=692 436=665
437=500 438=94 440=127 441=604 444=610 445=71 446=208
449=569 450=301 451=328 452=308 453=460 454=629 455=589
456=190 457=156 458=226 459=245 460=275 461=55 462=59

463=225 465=341 468=100 469=263 470=637 472=252 473=606
475=457 476=199 477=197 478=82 479=265 480=211 481=214
483=205 484=18 485=119 486=133 487=451 488=334 489=329
490=682 491=73 493=461 494=670 495=614 496=305 497=407
498=33 499=479

501=433 502=15 503=435 504=148 506=47 507=292 508=221
509=289 510=101 511=336 512=279 513=248 514=249 515=17
517=120 518=688 519=395 520=216 521=72 522=355 525=87
526=250 527=632 528=426 529=217 530=212 531=453 532=635
536=505 538=530 539=494 540=366 541=492 543=409 544=624
545=184 546=536 547=510 548=243 549=237 550=412 552=634
556=442 558=406 559=181 561=667 562=647 563=656 564=668
565=317 566=532 567=529 570=230 571=261 572=472 573=650
575=646 577=423 582=283 583=304 586=522 587=436 588=533
589=626 590=172 591=611 592=613 593=566 594=588 595=587
597=9 598=579 599=8

602=542 603=586 604=135 605=559 607=222 609=74 610=16
611=649 612=26 613=482 615=612 616=209 617=383 618=28
619=466 620=584 621=618 622=7 623=493 625=663 626=39
627=32 629=238 630=562 631=585 632=580 634=563 635=570
636=574 637=57 639=198 640=276 641=531 642=633 643=549
644=145 645=157 647=146 648=149 649=147 650=143 651=166
652=84 653=164 654=696 655=302 656=204 657=593 658=125
660=468 661=378 662=654 664=400 665=578 666=200 668=623
669=513 670=456 671=183 673=85 674=641 675=534 676=411
677=314 679=223 680=36 683=322 685=170 686=564 687=565
688=88 690=262 691=548 692=621 693=66 695=550 696=528
699=95

702=375 704=683 705=537 706=327 707=535 710=678 711=487
714=41 717=269 718=138 720=321 721=520 723=152 726=272
727=291 729=495 730=686 731=571 732=176 733=175 734=258
735=259 741=538 742=581 743=335 744=357 745=386 746=422
747=177 748=599 749=438 750=153 751=539 752=398 753=675
754=619 755=625 758=664 759=202 760=416 763=627 766=70

767=403 768=98 769=415 772=552 773=685 777=480 778=388
779=389 782=608 783=390 784=506 786=432 788=631 796=620
800=671

801=666 803=11 804=639 805=60 806=484 807=518 808=324
809=46 810=459 813=14 815=3 817=596 821=512 822=171 824=644
825=155 826=38 827=187 828=240 829=313 830=224 831=439
832=509 833=511 839=481 840=458 841=470 842=455 844=112
845=483 846=474 847=475 848=446 849=507 854=76 856=130
859=129 860=137 861=139 862=189 872=264 873=421 877=58
892=701

903=331 904=356 905=309 907=307 908=306 909=310 911=370
915=319 916=348 918=131 920=323 924=360 927=354 929=376
930=345 931=114 932=316 933=392 939=111 941=315 942=380
943=384 944=300 945=297 946=349 947=287 948=154 949=220
950=213 951=582 957=515 959=418

BIBLIOGRAPHY

Basak, Radhagovinda. *The Prākrit Gāthā-Saptaśatī. Compiled by Sātavāhana King Hāla.* Bibliotheca Indica 295. Calcutta 1971.

Boccali, G., Sagramoso, D., Pieruccini, C. *Hala—le settecento strofe (Sattasai).* Bibliotheca Indiana 3. Brescia 1990.

Dundas, Paul. *The Sattasaī and Its Commentaries. Pubblicazioni di "Indologica Taurinensia"* XVII. Torino 1985.

Patwardhan, M.V. *Hāla's Gāhākosa (Gāthāsaptaśatī) with the Sanskrit commentary of Bhuvanapāla.* Part 1 (Prakrit Text Series no.21), Ahmedabad 1980, Part 2 (B.L.Series no.5), Delhi 1988.

Tieken, Herman. "A Formal Type of Arrangement in the Vulgata of the *Gāthāsaptaśatī* of Hāla." *Studien zur Indologie und Iranistik* 4 (1978), 111–130.

Id. *Hāla's Sattasaī. Stemma and Edition (Gāthās 1–50), with Translation and Notes.* Leiden 1983.

Id. "Hāla's *Sattasaī* as a Source of Pseudo-Deśī Words." *Bulletin d'Études Indiennes* 10 (1992), 221–267.

Id. "Prākṛt Poetry: Hāla's *Sattasaī*." *Indian Horizon. Special Issue: Sanskrit Literature.* 44/4 (1995), 61–71.

Id. "Middle-Indic *tuppa*, Tamil *tuppu*, and the Region of Origin of Some Śvetāmbara Jaina Texts." *Bulletin d'Études Indiennes* 13–14 (1995–96), 415–429.

Id. *Kāvya in South India: Old Tamil Caṅkam Poetry.* Groningen 2001.

Weber, Albrecht. *Über das Saptaçatakam des Hāla. Abhandlungen für die Kunde des Morgenlandes.* V. Band, No. 3. Leipzig 1870.

Id. "Zum Saptaçatakam des Hāla." *Zeitschrift der Deutschen Morgenländischen Gesellschaft* 28 (1874), 345–436.

Id. *Das Saptaçatakam des Hāla. Abhandlungen für die Kunde des Morgenlandes.* VII. Band, No. 4. Leipzig 1881.

Id. Über Bhuvanapāla's Commentar zu Hāla's Saptaçatakam. *Indische Studien. Beiträge für die Kunde des indischen Altherthums.* XVI, Leipzig 1883, 1–204.

Id. "Idylles villageoises de l'Inde—les sept cents strophes de Hāla." *Revue International (Florence)* V (1884), 289–316.

www.ingramcontent.com/pod-product-compliance
Lightning Source LLC
Chambersburg PA
CBHW021856230426
43671CB00006B/410